KU-491-228

Alphonse Allais

# A WOLF IN FROG'S CLOTHING

The Best of Alphonse Allais
selected, translated and introduced by Miles Kington

A METHUEN HUMOUR CLASSIC

First published in Great Britain in 1977
by Chatto and Windus Ltd

This paperback edition first published in 1983
by Methuen London Ltd
11 New Fetter Lane, London EC4P 4EE

Copyright © Miles Kington 1976, 1983

ISBN 0 413 52680 1

Made and printed in Great Britain by
Richard Clay (The Chaucer Press) Ltd
Bungay, Suffolk

# CONTENTS

# INTRODUCTION TO THE PAPERBACK EDITION

Messrs. Methuen are reissuing this collection of Alphonse Allais stories in paperback under the impression that it is to introduce him to a wider public. Not so. The main purpose is to give me a chance to rewrite my introduction to the hardback.

When I wrote the introduction for the original edition of this collection (published by Chatto and Windus) with the title *The World of Alphonse Allais*, I made three bad mistakes.

I went on and on about how funny Allais was.

I tried to analyse his humour.

I ended up with an introduction much longer than any of the pieces in the book, rather as the Extras column sometimes outshines all the batsmen in an England side.

The first mistake was the worst, I think. There's something in human psychology which resents being told how great a film, play or book is. At least, when I follow up rave reviews I always come away thinking: Well, it wasn't *that* great. Whereas if I am told that something is not half bad, I often come away thinking how great it is.

Alphonse Allais is not half bad.

There is no point in analysing humour, because telling someone why a thing is funny will not make him laugh at it – on the contrary, it is more likely to stop him laughing.

And the length of the introduction came about, I think, because I hoped that people who enjoyed the book would want to know everything there was to know about the author. This was a mistake. The main purpose of information in an introduction is to provide facts for a book reviewer to parade as his own knowledge.

So this introduction will be shorter, unanalytical and modest in its claims. As it is, I have already gone on at greater length than Allais himself did. When he issued a collection called *The Squadron's Umbrella*, he wrote the following pithy note to readers:

'Some explanation of the title is in order.

'1. The umbrella, that useful modern device, is not mentioned in this book.

'2. The role of the cavalry squadron in modern warfare is much debated at the moment. Not by me, though.'

\*    \*    \*

I first came across the name of Alphonse Allais in a book by Roger
Shattuck called *The Banquet Years*, nearly twenty years ago. This
was a dazzling study of four of the main talents of turn-of-the-
century Paris – Jarry, Satie, Douanier Rousseau and Apollinaire –
and Allais's name cropped up in each section, referred to as if he
were some kind of court jester of the period. I came across a
paperback selection of his pieces six months later in Hachette and
bought it out of idle curiosity. An hour later I was hooked, and
started collecting his few and far between books.

One result of this was that on the odd occasions that publishers
asked me if I had ever thought of doing a book, I always used to
suggest doing a set of translations from Alphonse Allais. They backed
away from the idea of publishing an obscure French humorist as
hastily as if I had suggested doing a survey of sheep's diseases in
medieval Finland. In fact, there might never have been a book at all
if I had not in the early 1970s written off to the head of BBC Radio 3
in a fit of unusual energy suggesting lots of talks I could do for them.
One of the many ideas was a short series on unfashionable humorists,
and one of the names mentioned as an example was Allais.

Radio 3 wrote back immediately to reject all my ideas, but to
inquire curiously who this Alphonse bloke was. I explained cautiously
that he was the funniest writer France ever produced, or to put it
another way, not half bad. They cautiously commissioned a short
talk from me on Allais, which duly went out on Boxing Day 1973. In
the next fortnight I received letters from *four* different publishers
suggesting that I do a book of Allais material for them. I plumped for
Chatto and Windus for no better reason than that the Chatto man
who wrote to me was D. J. Enright, whose verse I like very much,
and in 1976 the book duly came out.

This may not tell you much about Allais, but it illustrates two
points which it is vital for young writers to know.

1. If you want to get a talk on Radio 3, it *has* to be about
someone they have never heard of. Make someone up, if necessary.
In fact many even of my closest friends believed for a long while
that I had made Alphonse Allais up.

2. If you want to get a book commissioned, the publisher is the last
person you go to. Get the idea mentioned elsewhere first and then the
publishers will chase after you, terrified at the prospect of missing the
boat. Alternatively, achieve something else first. Edward Heath had
to become Prime Minister before he could get published, though it is
not normally necessary to go to such lengths.

*        *        *

*The World of Alphonse Allais* was quite well reviewed and sold modestly well, at which point D. J. Enright revealed to me that within Chatto the book had always been known as 'Enright's folly'. But the interesting thing is that all the people I have met since then who bought and read the book have almost without exception treated him as their own private discovery, much as I had done in the 1960s. I was, for instance, interviewed by Stephen Pile for Atticus in *The Sunday Times* in late 1982 and I found to my delight that he much preferred to talk about Alphonse Allais's writings than to discuss mine, which was exactly how I felt. There is a flavour in Allais which is different from any flavour and which, given the right circumstances, is totally addictive.

To try and say why would involve committing the three mistakes of my original introduction.

*             *             *

Allais was not a cult in his own day. He was widely popular, the Beachcomber or Leacock of his time, but besides having a talent equal to theirs he also had the luck of being born at the right moment.

The moment was October 20, 1854, and the place Honfleur, which then was a beautiful unspoilt Norman fishing port, full of tile-hung houses and little backways, as it is to this day. It lies on one side of the Seine estuary, with the huge modern port of Le Havre on the other; in Allais's day (see his story 'A Tactical Error') you could catch a ferry from Le Havre to Honfleur, whereas now-adays – such is progress – you have to drive fifteen miles inland from Le Havre, cross the Tancarville Bridge and come fifteen miles back again.

Allais's father was the local pharmacist and Alphonse went for the local education at the same local school which was attended a few years later by Erik Satie. (Odd that two such quirky creators should come from the same solid bourgeois origins.) But it was not being born in Honfleur in 1854 that was lucky for Allais; it was being sent to Paris in the 1870s to complete a pharmaceutical education, for he arrived just at the moment when the first stirrings were being felt of the fermentation which would produce the champagne years of the Belle Epoque of *fin-de-siècle* Paris. Bohemia was just shifting from the Left Bank to Montmartre. The first ever cabaret, the Chat Noir, was just being set up in Montmartre. And new talent was being sought to provide it with entertainment.

The upshot was that Alphonse Allais never completed his pharmaceutical studies but found himself writing cabaret entertainments, devising sketches for other performers and reciting his own monologues. His true *métier*, though, was not found until Rodolphe Salis, proprietor of the cabaret, decided to start a magazine also called the *Chat Noir*, to which Allais was one of the main contributors until its demise in 1890. It was here that he learnt the art of creating a small firework display in about a thousand words, dazzling the reader with an array of impossible ideas which linger on the retina long after the entertainment is over.

After 1890 he went on to write for two other humorous periodicals, *Le Journal* and *Le Sourire*, even becoming editor-in-chief of the latter, and becoming at the same time jester-in-chief of the 1890s. So much so that Lisa Appignanesi could write, in her history of *The Cabaret*: 'Allais was a consummate absurdist. From an ordinary phenomenon, simple sentiment or situation, he would logically deduce the looniest, most macabre and most unexpected result ... His humour kept all Paris, high and low, waiting breathlessly for the paper which would carry his next tale.'

\* \* \*

Well, let me mention a few of his achievements. Allais was among other things the first man in history to paint an abstract picture. In the 1890s it was a common criticism of modern painters that they could not paint or draw; so Allais's circle decided to hold an exhibition by people, mostly writers, who genuinely could not paint or draw. Allais's contribution to this show, which they called the *Salon des Incohérents*, was a large, completely black rectangular canvas. It was entitled 'Negroes Fighting in a Cave at Night'. Encouraged by the success of this trail-blazing work, he followed it with six others, among them a totally white rectangle called 'Anaemic Young Girls Going to their First Communion through a Blizzard' and a red composition entitled 'Apoplectic Cardinals Harvesting Tomatoes by the Red Sea.'

He also invented a perfect method for being called early at a hotel without being rudely disturbed. It was to arrange an early morning call for the room on either side of you, and to be gently woken by the sound of your neighbours' protest. (Once it almost misfired; one of his neighbours obediently rose and dressed, paid his bill and left. Having been roused by the dim sound of fury through the other wall, Allais found the first man on the station platform half an hour later, still muttering to himself in a puzzled sort of way: 'I do wish I could remember why I had to make an early start.')

He died on October 28, 1905.

*          *          *

His life was uneventful. All the truly amazing things happened in his writing.

*          *          *

The one truly amazing thing that happened to me during the translating of my favourite Allais pieces was that I met someone who had known him, which came as some relief at a time when I was beginning to suspect that I really had made him up.

Not that I ever went looking for old friends of Allais. After all, the odds against finding anyone who might have known him were ludicrous – it would be easier, given the dates, to find old friends of Mahler or Henry James. All I did was go on a sort of sentimental pilgrimage to Honfleur in October 1975, to mark the seventieth anniversary of his death, and to see if anyone else was celebrating it. Well; they weren't. The town hall was totally unaware of his deathdate, and the only marks of respect in Honfleur were the usual; a back street named after him and a perfunctory 'Here was born Alphonse Allais' plaque.

Instead, I went to the Boudin museum – Boudin was another local boy made good – and happened to mention my pilgrimage to the young director of the gallery.

'I think you're in luck,' he said. 'We have an oldest inhabitant who remembers Alphonse Allais.'

And so, by God, they did. His name was Henry Couespel, and he was 94 years old, which made him 24 years old when Allais died. The reason he could remember Allais at all was that his own father had been a pharmaceutical supply merchant, supplying the raw materials for Allais's father's shop, and young Henry had often gone round there as the messenger boy between the two. So he had sometimes seen Alphonse when the latter came back from Paris to stay for a while.

'I'll be totally honest with you,' said Henry Couespel when I sat in his small, dark but very neat first floor flat. 'I am an old man and old men always exaggerate. They tell you what you want to hear and they make things up. But I can, truthfully, only re-member three things about Alphonse Allais and I will tell you those three things – after that, believe nothing that I say.'

They had never really known that Alphonse Allais was a famous writer, Couespel told me, not, at least, until after the Great War. All they knew when he came back to stay in Honfleur was that he worked for some paper or other in Paris.

'During his visits he used to spend most of his time wandering round the old port wearing a straw boater and carrying an old Norman peasant's walking stick' (I couldn't catch the local word for this) 'or sitting in a café. He always struck me as very introvert – *renfermé* – and as having rather highly coloured cheeks. That was because he drank, you know, drank too much. Absinthe, of course. He once invited me into the café for a drink with him, which was a great honour for me as a young lad.

'He always had a reputation as a great joker. I remember once he was in the butcher's shop overlooking the port and the butcher, who was a big, simple man, said to him: "Look, M. Allais, they've opened one of the lock gates into the inner basin, but kept the other closed. What on earth have they done that for?" "Easy," said Allais. "They want to half-empty the basin."'

M. Couespel chuckled at this.

'Of course, I read a lot of his stories after he died, and I found that a lot of the things he described had really happened. Do you remember that story called "Les Zèbres"?'

I did. It is not in this book, but it is an account of a wild practical joke about painting horses with black and white stripes and spreading a story about zebras and other animals escaping from a touring circus. Like most practical jokes, it was probably funnier at the time.

'Well, it was all true. He and a friend did it. I can remember it actually happening.'

While I was still marvelling that I should be in the presence of someone who had talked to Allais himself, Couespel let drop the ultimate one-up remark.

'Of course, I knew his parents much better.'

Six months after I returned to London, I got a letter from M. Couespel. 'You know I said I could only remember three things about Alphonse Allais? Well, I have remembered a fourth. He amused us once very much by writing a letter home from London and saying: "They are curious people, these English. Many of their public areas are named after famous British *defeats*. Trafalgar Square, Waterloo Place, etc.!"'

*        *        *

I didn't really learn anything about Allais from Henry Couespel worth knowing, or anything I didn't know already. His contemporaries have recorded that he was withdrawn and seldom smiled, that he drank, that he waited until the last moment for deadlines and would often sit in a café writing, with messengers coming screaming for copy. I know journalists like that today.

I have only mentioned Henry Couespel at length because he is the only living proof I have that Allais really existed.

Or was. Henry Couespel, too, died a few years ago.

*          *          *

Apart from that, I only hope that you enjoy the book, and remember that he is even better in the original. If you want to know more about him, write to me c/o Methuen, and I will send you a copy of the original introduction.

Miles Kington
London 1982

### A Note on the Translation

The main problem that a translator of Allais has to face is that he is untranslatable. It is almost impossible to transfer humour from one language to another. The rhythms of French are very different from those of English. Allais was a stylist who did tricks with French that cannot be done with English, any more than a genuine French loaf can be cooked from English flour.

So the best that can be done is to provide a version that suggests Allais's Frenchness, retains a period flavour and changes gear when the original does, while at the same time remaining fluent, not wooden. I have done this as best I could. I am not a professional translator; I am a professional humorous journalist with a degree in French and a big dictionary. Ideally, one should take as long to develop an English style for Allais as he himself did in French, but the publishers indicated to me they were not prepared to wait twenty years.

A few points.

Allais, like most Frenchmen, loved a good pun and rather liked a bad pun. Many of them occur in his made-up names (his American friend called Harry Covayre, for example) and all these I have left as he wrote them, for the reader to pick up for himself. His other puns I have either provided English substitutes for or, doubtless, failed to notice.

I have sometimes been deliberately anachronistic and used English slang terms which did not exist in his day. This is because many of the French slang terms he uses still exist, whereas the Victorian English equivalents have died. It seems better to recreate the original effect rather than create the original substance.

Occasionally he makes up words; sometimes prophetically. In one piece I use the word 'ecological'. This did exist in English at the time, but the word Allais used in French was his own invention 'géophile', which means *friend of the earth*.

From time to time I felt it was absolutely necessary to omit small passages, run paragraphs together, drop forgotten references and condense long-winded denouements. Not very often, though.

My only yardstick in selecting the pieces was to make them varied – to cover as many subjects as possible, while illustrating the different ways in which he used his cool, curiously modern style. I included 'The Doctor' as an example of the kind of cabaret sketch used at Le Chat Noir (it is dedicated to the actor who performed it). And 'Commercial Interlude' I thought worth using, as it reads like a good modern radio sketch. I find it impressive that they were writing good radio sketches in the 1890s.

Miles Kington

*This book is dedicated to Alphonse Allais, who wrote it.*

# HOW I BECAME A JOURNALIST

I hadn't been very long at my Jesuit college before I became totally disgusted by the vile, decadent goings-on there and decided to have nothing more to do with the ecclesiastical career my parents had planned for me. But after I had finally succeeded in escaping from the establishment, I was faced with another agonising problem. How to earn my living. A scientific examination of my pockets revealed the presence of a small deposit of copper and a few traces of silver. There was no sign of either gold or paper. Things looked grim.

Luckily, I bumped into an old friend who told me:

'It so happens I know a printer who is very keen to start a small local paper. As he is almost totally unable to spell, he is looking for an editor who is on speaking terms with the finer points of punctuation and allied cultural matters. Think you could do it?'

'I have a strange, overpowering feeling,' I told him, 'that I am the right man for the job.'

'Right, come on, I'll introduce you.'

The man in question turned out to be a big, fat, jolly printer with a fine moustache, going slightly grey. He greeted me quite disarmingly.

'Can you write good local news items?' he said.

Mentally, I shrugged my shoulders.

The telepathic printer would not take this for an answer.

'No, no, I don't mean the kind of boring local news you get in the usual provincial rag. What I want in *my* newspaper is local news with a difference!'

'Why not try me?'

'All right. Come and sit at my desk over here, and write me a news item for this headline: *Pipe-Smoker's Extreme Carelessness*.'

Not five minutes later I handed him the following story.

### PIPE-SMOKER'S EXTREME CARELESSNESS

The parish of Montsalaud was the scene last night of a tragic accident caused by a pipe-smoker's carelessness.

A local clog-maker was returning home about ten, smoking a pipe which gave off a constant shower of sparks.

He chose to come back through the small pine wood belonging

to the Marquise of Chaudpertuis, not realising that the slightest spark might ignite the dry twigs and fir cones lying in profusion all around him.

While thus walking along smoking his pipe, he suddenly stopped with a cry. For there beside the path lay two poor children asleep, entwined in each other's arms and shivering with cold.

Being a kind-hearted fellow, the clog-maker woke the children up and helped them build a big bonfire in the middle of the wood to get them warm again, then went on his way.

Unfortunately, the fire had been badly lit and soon went out. The bodies of the two children were found this morning. They had died of cold.

*          *          *

'Marvellous!' cried my new boss. 'That's what I call local news with a difference! Shake on it, young man!'


# MOTHERS-IN-LAW ARE THE NECESSITY OF INVENTION

Recently I received a letter from one of the most eminent scientists in France, bearing information which I think should be available to all my readers and indeed to all humanity. Here it is in full.

My dear Alphonse,

I enjoyed reading your fascinating case history of the mother-in-law who was frightened to death by a stuffed lion specially fitted out with flashing eyes and mechanically recorded roars.

As you know, it is no longer possible to be prosecuted for crimes committed over twenty years ago, so I now feel free to write and tell you how I brought about *my* mother-in-law's death, the twentieth anniversary of which I recently celebrated. The method I used was quite foolproof and needs only a little scientific knowledge, so if you care to offer the hospitality of your column to an account of my experience, I am sure many of your readers will be able to profit from it.

Although I had only been married a few months, I had already conceived a loathing for my mother-in-law which was enough to turn the mildest of men (I refer to myself) into a monster of ravening revenge. The question I kept asking myself was not 'Can I bring myself to do away with her?' (the answer to that was, Yes, and the sooner the better) but '*How* shall I do away with her?'

You see, I have never lost a lingering respect for our police force and, given the choice, I always prefer to avoid a direct confrontation with their crack troops.

And the trouble with killing anyone, even a mother-in-law, is that however discreetly it is done it tends to lead to a social call from a police sergeant, even an inspector or two.

So my method would have to be so completely waterproof as to baffle the finest sleuths in the whole of France, as they say in the sort of books where they say that sort of thing.

Well, I am a chemist by training, and it was to chemistry I eventually turned in my darkest hour.

I should tell you, by the way, that during the summer months my mother-in-law never wore anything but cotton.

She went around swathed from head to foot in cotton.

She was *mad* about cotton.

'Cotton,' she used to say at every opportunity, 'is the only really healthy material there is.'

And it was this that gave me my idea.

One fine day I crept up to her room as stealthily as an Apache burglar and spirited away an entire set of her clothes. Stockings, pants, skirt, blouse, everything. Clutching them tightly I stole off to my little private laboratory where I spent the rest of the day transforming them, by a fairly simple and common process, into guncotton.

The next step was to wait for a really hot sunny day and then so to arrange it that my dear mother-in-law found herself wearing that same set of chemically treated, highly dangerous garments.

And so it came to pass, in due course.

It was a sizzling hot day.

She went out into the garden and sat on a bench to read a trashy novel.

I crept up behind her armed with an extremely powerful lens and ruthlessly focussed the sun's rays on her.

It didn't take long – there was a scream, a searing flash like lightning, then . . . nothing.

At the inquest, the forensic scientist could find only one theory to fit the known facts. My mother-in-law must have been a secret alcoholic and subject to some strange, unknown form of spontaneous combustion.

I hardly thought it was my place to contradict an expert.

yours etc

X

(Member of the *Académie des Sciences*)

# A CHRISTMAS STORY

At Christmas time, about three years ago, I found myself detained by chance in a small prison in Yorkshire, awaiting trial on charges of theft, swindling and blackmail. (Thereby hangs a long and shameful story, which I would rather not go into as it brings back painful memories.) It wasn't so much being in prison that upset me; it was being there at that particular season, because I have always loved Christmas. Ah, Christmas! The time for all children to gather round the fireplace and enjoy themselves! The time for all grown-ups to gather under the mistletoe and ditto!

But Christmas in England is a very private affair, and nowhere more so than in Yorkshire, where things are very far removed from our own social junketings in Paris. At least, it felt very far to me.

Where privacy was concerned, I had no cause for complaint. My cell was private enough, perhaps even too private. The gaoler had . . .

Ah, I had forgotten all about my gaoler. What a curious fellow he was! An old soldier, an ex-Horse Guard who had lost a leg in the Ashanti War. And as he had only joined the Horse Guards to wear the grand uniform in the first place, he had gone on wearing it through thick and thin, even after he had lost his leg and changed his job. I could never help smiling at the sight of him, with one leg made of wood and the other spurred, booted and trousered. It was funny, yet it was touching too.

Meanwhile, Christmas was coming closer and closer.

And there I was, I who had been invited to spend the Christmas holiday in the Faroe Isles, with a missionary and his family!

All my readers must know what it is like to be in prison, but how many of you have ever been in prison in snowy weather? I know nothing worse. All sound vanishes utterly; sweet sound, the only thing that keeps you in touch with the outside world. When snow falls you can no longer see or hear anything.

It fell relentlessly that year, hard, thick, slanting, until my poor little cell was completely muffled and deadened. And there was one noise which I missed more than any other, out of all those I had come to know and cherish in my captivity: the sound of my gaoler walking across the main prison yard. First the dull *clunk* of the wooden leg on the paving stones, then the triumphant *smack* of his boot with the jingling of his spur. Clunk, smack, clunk, smack, and so on alternately. All gone, all gone.

Did it mean that the old Horse Guard no longer ventured out into the prison yard? Or was he still walking across, but in complete silence? I worried about it endlessly, as prisoners are wont to when they have absolutely nothing else to do.

Then Christmas Eve arrived. It became dark, but I could not bring myself to go to bed. I could hear the bells ringing, first in the town, then in all the little surrounding villages. The village church bells were all muffled by the snow, muted by the distance and so evocative that I felt my eyes brimming with tears. I always feel like crying when I hear the far-off sound of bells in the countryside.

'Come in!' I said, startled out of my reverie.

Somebody had knocked at the door.

It opened, and in came a pink and white maiden of about fifteen, carrying a little basket in one hand and a large spray of mistletoe in the other.

'Good evening, sir,' she said.

'Good evening, miss,' I replied, also in English.

She went on:

'Well, do you remember the last time you met me?'

'Of course,' I said. 'In one of Kate Greenaway's books, wasn't it?'

'No, never.'

'Oh. In a drawing by Robert Caldecott, then?'

'No, wrong again.'

I fell silent.

'Have you *really* forgotten?' she said crossly. 'It was in London last year. Don't you remember? You saved me from certain death. I was walking across Trafalgar Square when suddenly one of the bronze lions charged furiously at me, roaring loudly. I ran away as fast as I could. You were sitting on the top deck of a passing omnibus. You leant down and with one powerful arm snatched me from the clutches of the predatory beast. Cheated of his prey, the lion slunk back to his normal place and struck once again the artistic pose the sculptor had designed for him.'

I racked my brain, but could recall nothing remotely like that which had ever happened to me. She was quite firm, though.

'You *must* remember! It was the *Bull and Gate* bus. You were on your way to see your friend Lombardi at the Villa Chiavenna.'

Faced with such a wealth of circumstantial detail, I had to give in and agree.

So she took a large plum pudding out of her basket, together with several bottles of English ale, and we proceeded to make merry.

When dawn came, she slipped away, taking with her my heart and the empties.

Ever since then, I have often tried to remember taking part in that curious episode in Trafalgar Square.

I have always failed.

Nor, to tell the truth, can I remember ever having been in prison in Yorkshire with a wooden-legged gaoler, his pink and white daughter, a plum pudding and several bottles of ale.

Is it not curious how, in this life, we forget so much?


# THE LANGUAGE OF FLOWERS

If a man goes abroad to do some travelling and then returns after, say, a couple of hundred years, he won't be surprised to find that all the local landmarks have meanwhile fallen into ruin and become shadows of their former selves. These things do happen.

But I *was* surprised when exactly the opposite happened to me very recently. I had only been away five or six months from the stretch of coast which I call home, so I was staggered to find on my return that it is now dominated by an imposing medieval mansion which, I swear, was not there when I left and had certainly not been there during the Middle Ages. Like any good amateur detective, I immediately deduced that it was a forgery, and a recent one at that.

I don't mean that there is anything criminal about the place, of course. Ludicrous is a better word. It smells of fake antique all over, with its battered battlements, tottering towers, missing machicolations and its ogival windows protected by bars so thick they would defeat any barometer. It is, in short, a piece of lunacy.

As soon as I got home I asked about this weird addition to the landscape and was quickly brought up to date on the history of the neo-ancient monstrosity, as well as the history of its owner, who turns out to be none other than the ex-chiropodist of the Queen of Roumania. His name is Baron Lagourde (though he's about as much a baron as I am Father Superior of a Greek monastery) and he has made vast amounts of money deploying his delicate skills on the crowned feet of Europe. The only other thing worth telling you about the Baron (I'll stick to his title as it is the kind of thing that seems to please him) is that he is fat and common and ugly and appears to keep his brains in his feet.

And he has a wife, who comes from western Bulgaria. A small, dark woman, somewhat on the unkempt side, but I'll say this for her: she does have the gift of arousing thoughts of adultery in the opposite sex. To be quite frank, this female Bulgar de l'Ouest – or what in Paris we call a Bulgar St. Lazare – had not been in Normandy long before she started deceiving her husband with a constant stream of road menders. Road menders? Why road menders, I hear you ask? Why not rural postmen or diplomatic attachés? Ah, shall we ever know the mysteries of the female heart! Let me simply record that the baroness finds road menders particularly irresistible, and that she never manages to refuse their advances. Which is why, this last summer, the road from Trouville to Honfleur received so little love and attention. Unlike the road menders.

Anyway, it seems that the Baron Lagourde settled in this part of the country early this year and bought a superbly situated property with a spectacular view – the estuary of the Seine to his right, the promontory of Le Havre opposite and the open sea over to the west. And having secured such a prime estate, the royal ex-pedicure proceeded to stamp on it his own peculiar idea of aesthetics in general and of feudal interior decor in particular. Before you could say 'Jacques Robinson', a manor house had arisen, ready crumbled. He hired specialist workmen to give it that whiff of decay without which no modern stately home can ever seriously hope to be truly medieval. He left nothing to chance – he even ordered real skeletons, loaded with chains, to be cast into the lowest dungeons.

And the Baron might have been very happy in his pseudo-

Middle Ages if it had not been for the stubbornness of old man
Fabrice. But, sad to say, the more the Baron tried to make him see
reason, the more old man Fabrice dug his heels in. The trouble
was, you see, that old man Fabrice owned the next door field, a
long though not very wide meadow which ran right across the top
of the Baron's feudal domain and commanded an even more
splendid view than he had. It wouldn't have fetched more than
about 600 francs on the open market. Lagourde kindly offered
him 1,000 francs for it. Then, after a while, 1,100 francs. Finally,
at the end of a lot of haggling, a last offer of 2,000 francs.

'Ah, no, Baron,' said the sly old farmer, shaking his head. 'I
reckon it be worth a good deal more than that. I reckon it do be
worth a great deal more.'

But the Baron had no intention of going higher than 2,000 francs
and that, so far as he was concerned, was that.

Well, one day not so long ago (so I was told) the noble chiropodist was lolling atop one of his towers, idly scanning the horizon
through a magnificent pair of field glasses (made by Flammarion
Ltd., advt.) when he happened to focus on a yacht quite near the
coast and was amazed to observe the yacht's entire company of
lady and gentlemen guests assembled on the bridge, staring
through binoculars in *his* direction.

The thing that amazed him was that they were all doubled up
with laughter. Every now and again they swapped binoculars and
fell about laughing all over again. It was enough to make the
Baron feel vaguely offended. Could it, by any chance, be *his*
superb château they were laughing at?

That might not have been so bad were it not for the fact that
the same yacht reappeared the very next day and went through
the same performance, this time accompanied by two pleasure
boats whose passengers were unaccountably subject to the same
fits of uncontrollable laughter. And what made it even worse was
that every succeeding day after that more and more boats joined
in. They all slowed down as soon as they drew level with the
château. And they all had passengers on board who seemed equally
prone to this terrible laughing disease. Even the ordinary fishing
boats from Trouville, Villerville and Honfleur all seemed to contain
fishermen in the grip of some strange, manic laughing fit. In brief,
it soon became impossible for anyone to navigate past that particular stretch of coastline without going under with laughing sick-
ness.

The Baron went through progressive stages of anxiety, distress and finally palpable anguish until one morning he decided it was time to find out for himself what exactly was causing this unseemly mirth on the high seas. So he went down to the harbour, hired a boat and sped under full sail towards the spot where everyone else seemed to be enjoying themselves so much. Not fifteen minutes later his majestic manor house came into view, absolutely feudal in every detail and not in the least funny to look at. There was nothing amiss at all. What on earth could those idiots possibly have found to laugh at?

Then ... horror of horrors! The Baron could not believe his eyes! Anyone watching him closely would have seen such strenuous emotions as indignation, fury, outrage and many others closely related chasing across his face, leaving it a nasty crimson colour. There, before his very eyes ... but was it possible?

High above his manor house, plain for all to see, old man Fabrice's meadow lay in the sun like a vast green banner, but a banner with a strange device. For on it there was written a horrifyingly legible message in bright yellow, namely:

### THE BARON'S WIFE IS A WHORE!

The explanation was quite simple. The nasty old man had sown in his meadow a great quantity of those flowers known commonly as buttercups, and sown them according to this outrageous but unmistakable pattern. Old man Fabrice had said it with flowers on a vast scale.

The Baron stood rooted to the deck, stunned with horror and shame by the scandalous message picked out so prettily in light yellow against the dark green background of the field.

'The Baron's wife is a whore ... the Baron's wife is a whore ....' he repeated to himself, in a complete daze. It was only when he heard the crew laughing behind his back that he came out of his dream.

'Take me straight back to land!' he ordered, in the most feudal tone of voice he could muster in the circumstances.

When he had disembarked, he went to see the mayor at once.

'Mr. Mayor,' he said, 'I have been most grossly libelled in your district. It is your duty to uphold my honour. You must take immediate action.'

'Libel? What kind of libel, Baron?'

'Old man Fabrice has gone too far. He has written on his field that my wife ... my wife is a whore.'

'Written it ... on his field? I don't quite ....'

'Yes, written – with yellow flowers!'

Luckily, the mayor had known about Fabrice's ingenious idea for some time, or he might have been slightly puzzled by the Baron's complaint. So together they went off to see the author of the offending message, who only reacted with injured innocence to the charge.

'*Me*, Baron? *Me* write that your wife do be a whore? Now, how could you think me capable of such a thing? I don't know as when I've been so terrible offended.'

'Well, we'd better go and have a look,' sighed the mayor.

When they got to the field they could see that the buttercups did form some sort of pattern all right, but from where they stood it was quite impossible to make any sense out of it. They were far too close. (Exactly the same phenomenon has been observed in those flies who live in libraries and spend most of their life walking across printed pages, yet remain quite unable to decipher a single word.)

'I'm sure the Baron realises,' said old man Fabrice, 'that wild flowers grow much where they want to and don't ask nobody's permission. If we was held responsible for the way they grew . . .!'

'Well, Mr. Mayor,' growled the Baron, 'who are you going to believe?'

'I assure you, Baron, I am only too happy to take your word for it that you have been libelled, but if the libellous message can't be read in my area of jurisdiction, then it's not really up to me to deal with it. You said you had been insulted while out at sea; you should complain to the Admiralty!'

The Baron could foresee that complaining to the Admiralty about a libel case on land might be a complicated affair. He thought of a better way out.

'Well, you old bastard,' he said to Fabrice, 'how much do you want for your damned field?'

'Ah, now, Baron, you know right well I don't want to sell the field, but seeing as how you seem so set on it, well, I'll do you a favour and let you have it for a mere 10,000 francs. A fair old bargain it is, too. Not many fields you find with flowers that can spell all by themselves!'

And that very evening old man Fabrice's flowery prose vanished beneath the implacable scythe of the Baron's gardener, since when everything has been back to normal. I have one piece of advice for the Baron, though. If he is thinking of playing the same trick on Fabrice next year, he might as well forget the idea now. Old man Fabrice doesn't care a damn what anyone says about him.

# ANYTHING THEY CAN DO....

Little Madeleine Bastye might have been the most fascinating and desirable woman of the entire nineteenth century but for one small, annoying fault. She was incapable of taking a lover without immediately being unfaithful to him. For most people broadmindedness means taking one thing with another; for her it meant only taking one man with another.

When our story starts, her lover was a fine upstanding young man called Jean Passe (of the firm, Jean Passe et Desmeilleurs).

Not only was Jean Passe a decent sort, he was also a credit to the Paris business world. So of course he was determined to do the honourable thing by Madeleine.

Not so Madeleine. She was unfaithful to him at the first opportunity.

Jean was heartbroken.

'But what has he got that I haven't got?' he asked.

'He's so *handsome!*' sighed Madeleine.

'We'll see about that,' muttered Jean.

Love is strong! The will is all-powerful! When Jean came home that evening he had been transformed into the most handsome man in the world, beside whom the Archangel Gabriel would have looked as ugly as sin.

\*　　\*　　\*

The second time Madeleine was unfaithful to Jean, Jean asked Madeleine:

'And what has *he* got that I haven't got?'

'Money!' said Madeleine.

'Right,' gritted Jean.

And that very day he invented a cheap, simple, non-labour-intensive process for converting horse dung into the most exquisite plush velvet.

American manufacturers fought among themselves in an attempt to pour millions of dollars into his pockets....

\*　　\*　　\*

The third time Madeleine was unfaithful to Jean, Jean asked

Madeleine:

'And what has he got that *I* haven't got?'

'He's got a sense of humour, that's what,' said Madeleine.

'Right,' grunted Jean.

And he headed straight for the Flammarion bookshop to buy *Pas de Bile*, the latest collection of pieces by famed author Alphonse Allais. He read it from cover to cover, and back again, till he was so impregnated with the spirit of this unique book that Madeleine could hardly get to sleep at night for laughing.

\*          \*          \*

The fourth time Madeleine was unfaithful to Jean, Jean asked Madeleine:

'And *what* has he got that I haven't got?'

'Well . . .' said Madeleine.

She could not put it into words, but her blazing eyes said it for her. Jean understood.

'Right!' he cried.

\*          \*          \*

If this were a pornographic publication, I could now tell you what Jean did next and we could all enjoy ourselves. Sadly, it isn't and we can't.

\*          \*          \*

The fifth time Madeleine was unfaithful – oh, forget it . . .!

The hundred and fourth time Madeleine was unfaithful to Jean, Jean asked Madeleine:

'And what has he got that I *haven't* got?'

'He's very special,' said Madeleine. 'He's a *murderer*.'

'Is he now!' said Jean.

And he killed her.

It was about this time that Madeleine gave up being unfaithful to Jean.

# GHOST STORY

Christmas comes but once a year, and when it comes it brings roast chestnut sellers, chimney sweeps, Father Christmasses and all other seasonal nuisances. Not that I mind them too much; what I *do* object to is finding that the 21.22 train back to Paris suddenly starts vanishing at 20.17. And I told the station master so in no uncertain terms.

'This – is – absolutely – monstrous!'

It was no use. The tall, blond, vaguely retarded-looking station master simply said:

'Can't help that, sir. Winter timetable started yesterday. Sorry, sir.'

And that was that.

Luckily the friend I had been spending the weekend with in the country had brought me to the station in his carriage and stayed to see me off, so he promptly said:

'No problem at all, old chap. You must come back and stay the night with us. Plenty of spare beds, I'm glad to say.'

And off we jogged into the night again, drawn by his patient white mare. But by the time we finally got back to his house again the cold had bitten deep into our bodies and we decided that the only thing that could possibly arrest our falling temperatures was a generous injection of old Calvados. It did the trick all right, though I have to admit it took a whole bottle to do it. In mitigation, we did get some help from the lady of the house, not to mention her two daughters, who sipped away as if they had done it all their lives.

So there we were, sitting up late at night in the middle of the country. And when you sit up late at night in the middle of the country, what do you talk about? Of course you do. You talk about ghosts. So we started talking about ghosts.

'Oh, M. Allais, you shouldn't make fun of ghosts,' the elder daughter, Césarine, told me. 'They really do exist, you know.'

'Ah, but have you ever seen one?'

'Well, no . . . but I've heard one!'

'Really? Where was that?'

'Right here in this house. In the Pink Room.'

The rest of the family came to her defence. They had all heard noises coming from the Pink Room on different occasions, and always at night. Of course, it *might* have been the wind. Or the furniture cracking. On the other hand, it might not have been.

'Well,' I said firmly, '*I* have never seen a ghost and I would very much like to, so why not let me sleep in the Pink Room tonight?'

They greeted this proposal with a chorus of total horror, then readily fell in with my idea. So the ladies went off to make up a bed for me before retiring, while my host and I decided to sit up just a little while longer in the company of another bottle of very old Calvados, which in due course went to join its predecessor in that place from which no bottle ever returns. And it came to pass that while I was expounding to my host, in a less than coherent manner, my plans for the social reform of France, the the old grand-father clock whirred and struck half past eleven.

'Damn!' I thought. 'I'd better get to bed if I want to see my ghost.'

Now, when you over-indulge in fermented cider you tend to see things just that bit more clearly than usual and it suddenly occurred to me that it wouldn't be right to receive a ghost in a night shirt, especially if he turned out to be a well-born ghost. So, for purely social reasons you understand, I fell on to my bed fully clothed and passed out.

Then midnight struck. And the last echoes of the twelfth stroke had not yet died away in the empty air of the Pink Room when there came a sharp knocking at the door.

I started upright.

'Who's there?'

'The ghost.'

'Ah, yes, of course . . . sorry . . . do come in, please.'

I swear the door never moved, yet suddenly there stood before me a human form which – though absolutely lifelike – had no substance or corporeality at all, except for a black eye-patch over its left eye. This being the first time I had ever come face to face with an apparition I felt at some loss how to proceed, especially as the damned thing seemed in no hurry to open its mouth. I waited a bit. Nothing happened. So I said, rather lamely, I'm afraid:

'So you're the ghost, are you?'

'I am.'

'I see. Good. Right. Well . . . carry on, then.'

At this the ghost shrugged what were once his shoulders and an expression of inexpressible contempt flitted across the little patch of light he used to call his face.

'Is that really the best a haunted person can manage? *Carry on, then?* Honestly, it's hardly worth being a ghost if you can't elicit something wittier than that.'

That's better, I thought. Quite sensible, for a ghost. Trenchant, even.

'I'm sorry,' I said. 'Won't you sit down?'

'It's very kind of you, but I never sit down. We ghosts don't weigh anything, you know. So we never get tired and we never have to sit down.'

'That must be very handy.'

'It is. It's all the same to me whether I'm lying down, standing up or hovering in mid-air.'

'But what happens if you want to get somewhere else?'

'Same applies. Space has no meaning for me, you see. I'm here now, but if I wanted to, I could be in North Africa inside five minutes.'

'That's extraordinary. Apart from everything else, it must mean incredibly low running costs.'

'Of course it does – virtually nil. Just as well, considering that ghosts never seem to have any money.'

'You're not the only ones . . . Which reminds me. If you can really get around that fast, would you do me a little favour?'

'No trouble. Just name it.'

'The thing is, I have a little girl-friend I'm rather fond of who has just gone over to England for a while on doctor's orders. Change of climate, that sort of thing. Well, at the moment she's living in a little place just outside Brighton called Guadilquivir Cottage. If it's not too much trouble, I thought you might pop over there and see if she's getting on all right, behaving herself properly and so on.'

The ghost nodded, winked and vanished.

(I may say that I had absolutely no worries on that score. She was one of those rare girls who are not only beautiful but as trustworthy and honourable as they are beautiful.)

Before two minutes were up, the ghost was back again.

'Well?' I said.

'Well!' he said. '*Well!* Some girl-friend, that's all I can say!'

'Just what do you mean by that?' I said icily.

'Put it this way. You're not exactly sober yourself, are you? No,

you're not. But the way *she* is, she makes you look as sober as
a . . . .'

'Watch it!'

'All right, put it another way. Your girlfriend, at this very
moment, is knocking back her third bottle of plonk, in the company
of four Horse Guards officers who are wearing sabres, berets and –
are you listening to me? – not a stitch more.'

'*What!* And what about her?'

'Oh, she's still got the odd garment on. Not for long, though,
I'd guess.'

'You bastard!' I shouted. 'You damned liar!'

And I let him have a tremendous punch right on the jaw. Sadly,
I'd forgotten that he was not only a damned liar but also a super-
natural apparition. The result being that my fist travelled straight
through him and crashed agonisingly against the all-too-solid
moulding of an ancient Normandy wardrobe. The pain made me
cry out loud; the sound of which woke me up.


# LIGHTHOUSES


L'Eure is probably one of the few inland *départements* in France,
and certainly the only one, to possess a maritime lighthouse. But
how it ever came to acquire it, what vile intrigues were necessary
to gain permission, what depths of corruption were plumbed in its
construction, I do not know and have not the slightest wish to
know.

Of course, any petty bureaucrat will point out that it is quite
logical to place a powerful lighthouse inland on raised ground and
still have it perfectly visible from the sea if it is not too far away. I
know that. All I am saying is that when you live in Honfleur as I
do (home of the founders of Quebec, 1608) and a friend comes to
stay as he did last weekend and says he would like to visit a really
good, modern lighthouse, as he also said last weekend, it is most
humiliating to have to take him into a neighbouring *département*
whose main idea of navigational daring is to sail up the river to
Pont-Audemer.

Not that I didn't enjoy the journey to the lighthouse. Far from
it. It's a delightful road all the way, lined with charming old ladies
knitting in the sunshine and even more charming young girls, going

to the well to fill what they quaintly call their 'boocket'. What treasures they are, these northern nymphs, these Norman beauties! (I'm thinking of one in particular, who lives just this side of Ficquefleur.)*

The lighthouse is at Fatouville. When you get there the head keeper comes out to welcome you and to remind you constantly of his exalted rank. You climb up a winding staircase, which has no less than x number of steps in it. (I forget the exact number now, though I knew once. Ah, well – which famous French writer was it said: 'I think, therefore I forget'? I don't remember offhand.) And when you get to the top you are rewarded with a superb view, as they say, a breathtaking circular panorama containing an extraordinary number of square miles, though I have long since forgotten exactly how many, perhaps because I could never quite understand how a circular panorama could contain square miles.

'What is that lighthouse over there called?' said one of the visitors, pointing to the distant river Seine.

'That?' said the keeper, obviously offended. 'You call *that* a lighthouse, madame?'

The visitor turned bright red, momentarily confusing the nearby shipping.

'That is not a lighthouse; it is merely a beacon.'

He did however condescend to tell us the name of the beacon. I only wish I could remember it.

When we were sated with the landscape we climbed down exactly the same number of steps we had so recently ascended and were asked to sign the visitors' book. Modestly I concealed my identity and signed myself 'M. le Président de France'. And in the column headed 'Comments' I wrote:

'. . . . . . . . . . . . . . . . . . . . . . . . . . . . . . . . . . . .'

Very apt, I thought at the time, even if the exact wording has now slipped my memory.

We were just about to get in our carriage for the return journey when we were approached by a strange little man, of no particular age, who asked if we were going to Honfleur. We admitted that we were and, when he requested to be allowed to come with us, said we would be delighted. As soon as we had set off, he revealed that he was an inventor, specialising as it happened in revolutionary designs for lighthouses.

'You mean, a revolving lighthouse?' I said.

* I have since found out that she is Parisian born and bred. No matter, I still love her.

'Ah, you're interested in lighthouse design, then, are you?'

'Well, yes,' I said, 'and then again, no.'

'Well, you should be, because it's a fascinating subject.'

I should have told him that I did not feel like being fascinated by any subject just at the moment, not when we were travelling along such a magnificent coastline in beautiful soft golden October weather, which I would much rather have enjoyed than his conversation. But there was no stopping him.

'You see, conventional lighthouses are all right in clear weather, but when is the weather *really* clear?'

'Well, I've often . . .'

'Never! Not *really* clear. So . . .'

'But you can use a fog-horn then.'

'Fog-horn? Phooey. No sailor in a fog has the vaguest idea where the sound of a fog-horn is coming from. He'll always be at least 30° out. So I have invented something better. You see, if sound is so deceptive, it stands to reason that what you need is a smellhouse. Shall I explain?'

'I think you'd better.'

'Instead of lights we ought to be using smells. Every lighthouse should have its own agreed smell. I visualise a lemon lighthouse, a carnation lighthouse, a coffee lighthouse and so on all round the coast. If you had a powerful vaporiser mounted on top of the smellhouse, it would blow the odour far out to sea. So, in foggy weather the captain of a ship would only need to take a quick sniff and find, for example, that there were cloves to the N.N.W. and wallflowers to the S.E. He would check his chart and plot his bearing exactly. You see?'

'Splendid! I think you have overlooked one thing though. The most powerful smell you can arrange is a good local cheese, which would give you different flavours in different parts of France. But lighthouses are often battered by terrible storms and cut off from vital supplies of food. What would you say when you found that an awful disaster at sea had been caused by a starving lighthouse keeper who had been obliged to eat his lighthouse?'

The inventor gave me a queer look and mercifully kept quiet for the rest of the journey.

# A CAREFUL CRIMINAL

With the help of an ingenious gadget (made in America) similar to that used for opening tins of food, the lawbreaker made two incisions in the metal shutters of the shop, one vertical, one horizontal, and both starting from the same point.

He put forth a strong hand and pulled the triangle of metal thus created towards him as easily as if it had been made of tinfoil.

(He was strong, as lawbreakers go.)

When he had squeezed through into the little space on the other side, he found himself facing the main shop door.

Carefully keeping the glass part of the door in position with a rubber suction cup (made in America) he proceeded to cut through it with a Cape diamond.

There was no further bar to his entry. Once inside, he began very calmly and methodically piling into a convenient bag as many jewels and precious stones as he could find, for jewels, as you know, combine the twin advantages of great value and modest volume.

His work was almost over when the owner of the shop, a certain M. Josse, appeared at the far end of the room with a candle in one hand and a revolver in the other.

Very courteously the lawbreaker greeted him with the affable remark:

'Hello there – I was just passing by and thought it would be rude not to drop in and say hello.'

The goldsmith, quite unsuspecting, came forward with outstretched hand and the lawbreaker swiftly plunged a sharp metal weapon (made in America) into his chest.

After which he finished loading his convenient bag with jewels and precious stones.

He was almost back in the street when a sudden thought struck him.

Retracing his steps, he returned to the shop counter and wrote a few words in large letters on a sheet of paper.

As he went out he pasted it on the shop front. And next morning the passers-by all read:

CLOSED OWING TO DEATH OF OWNER

# ST. PETER AND HIS CONCIERGE

If you imagine that the proceedings of the Académie Française are always dull and dreary, then you are much mistaken. I would not go so far as to recommend them as an alternative to an evening at the Moulin Rouge, but they certainly have their moments. During the last session, for instance, I especially enjoyed a learned speech by M. Clermont-Ganneau, an archaeologist and a gentleman, which proved beyond all doubt that concierges were in existence thousands of years ago and that documentary evidence had come to light about the one employed by St. Peter, the late lamented apostle.

M. Clermont-Ganneau has even discovered her name, which was Ballia, or more accurately Ba'aya, the Aramaic present participle feminine meaning 'a woman asking for more than she has got', which shows that concierges haven't changed much over the years.

Fired by M. Clermont-Ganneau's discovery and anxious to learn more, I remembered suddenly that the public library at Criqueboeuf near Villerville on the Channel coast has perhaps the richest collection of Aramaic manuscripts anywhere in the world.

I sprang into action at once . . . .

'Driver! How much would it cost to take me to Criqueboeuf?'

'Hmm . . . And back again?'

'Yes, please.'

'Will you be there long?'

'Just as long as it takes to consult a few Aramaic manuscripts.'

'Ah, in that case, jump in! I'm a bit of an archaeologist myself and I'm always glad to give a colleague a free ride. Perhaps you've read my "Report on Some Broken Egyptian Bottles of the Eleventh Dynasty"?'

'Not yet, actually.'

'Never mind, jump in and I'll tell you all about it as we go along.'

There's nothing like a bit of historical chit-chat about broken bottles to make a journey pass quickly, and before I knew where we were, we were in Criqueboeuf.

My hunch proved absolutely correct.

The manuscripts in the library were *full* of stuff about Peter and his concierge. And she turns out to have been typically bad-tempered, shrewish, demanding, gossipy and fussy. In short, she made his life hell and there was nothing he could do about it, being a good, forgiving apostle. He was also, as we know from the New Testament, a bit of a coward on occasion, and her flood of incessant nagging met no obstacle except the humble dykes of his boundless patience and constant generosity. Because every time he came back from a day's fishing, he would have a nice turbot for her, or a pair of lemon sole, or perhaps a basket of smelts or shrimps, and he would smilingly hand them over to the old crone. But Ba'aya had no time for his little acts of kindness; she always yelled:

'You get your filthy smelly boots off before you dare come in here, and go up the back way, because I've cleaned the front stairs once today and I'm not doing it again. You stink to high heaven of fish!'

And poor Peter always had to take his boots off and go up the back way.

The only time the apostle ever got angry was when she objected that all this fresh fish meant hours of extra work in the kitchen and why couldn't he just bring back some smoked salmon or a tin of sardines. That time he really let her have a piece of his mind.

Anyway, when St. Peter died in AD 65 in his well-known final appearance as a double act with St. Paul, he appeared in due course at the gates of Heaven and was personally welcomed by God the Father with a little good-natured teasing.

'Welcome, Peter! Nice to meet you at last! My son has told me so much about you.'

'Gosh, that's very nice of Him,' said Peter, a bit overcome by his reception.

'He tells me, though, that your behaviour on the Night of the Passion wasn't entirely impeccable.'

'Ah, yes, well, yes, I must admit that I wasn't up to my best that night. Bit of a bad show, I'm afraid.'

'Never mind, I don't blame you. You've made up for it since then, and I can never thank you enough for all the work you did for us at Antioch and Rome.'

'Oh, it was nothing, God. I'm sure you'd have done the same in my place, what? I mean . . . .'

'What I really want to know is this. As a reward for your life on earth, have you any special favour to ask up here?'

At which St. Peter's face took on a very thoughtful and not altogether Christian expression.

'Tell me,' he said, 'do you have a certain party named Ba'aya among your tenants up here?'

'I've no idea, but I can easily find out. Let's ask the archangel on duty.'

A little research revealed that the certain party named Ba'aya had not yet reached Heaven, being engaged on a transit period of 3,000 years in Purgatory.

'Three thousand years!' exclaimed Peter, a bit taken aback. 'You don't believe in half measures, do you, Holy Father?'

'What is three thousand years compared to eternity? I can see you have a lot to learn here, Peter.'

'Well, about my favour. What I'd like to know is, do you have a concierge up here in Heaven?'

'No, nothing like that. The gates of Heaven are guarded by whichever archangel with a flaming sword is on duty. Sometimes when there has been an epidemic or a big war we call out a few extra people, and when there are really big crowds arriving everyone has to work overtime, but things always get back to normal quickly. Why?'

'Because I would like to take over the job of looking after the gates of Heaven personally.'

'What a funny thing to ask!'

'I have my reasons.'

God smiled omnisciently to himself and said:

'All right, I grant your request. Archangel, hand over the keys of Heaven to this gentleman, will you?'

And for the last 1,818 years St. Peter has been gleefully anticipating the expression on Ba'aya's face when she turns up to be admitted to Heaven and sees her old tenant installed as concierge at the pearly gates.

He rubs his hands and says to himself:

'Only another 1,007 years to go!'

Which leaves him just about enough time to work out exactly what he is going to say to the old cow.

# THE POOR BASTARD AND
# THE GOOD FAIRY

Once upon a time there was a poor bastard. You know when something terrible or other happens to a friend of yours, and you say, 'Poor bastard'? Well, *all* those terrible things had happened to our hero. He had bad luck the way other people have bad breath. Like a great black cloud it hovered over him night and day. Though he didn't know it, he had set several world records for bad luck. Poor bastard.

There came a day when he decided to empty his pockets and add up his entire worldly possessions. It didn't take very long. The total came to 1 fr. 90 (one franc ninety centimes) which was just about enough to get him through the day. How on earth would he get through tomorrow, though? Poor bastard.

Nothing dismayed, he carefully dabbed some black ink on to the worn seams of his overcoat and sallied forth in the vain hope of finding work. The overcoat had once been black, but Time, the Great Dyer, had gradually changed it into a green overcoat, despite which the poor bastard always thought of it as his best black coat. His top hat had been black too, once, but had slowly become dark red over the years. (Are not the ways of Nature inscrutable?) Worn together, the red top hat and green overcoat were somewhat eye-catching – the red looked redder and the green looked even greener. When he went out in what he thought of as his tidy black clothes, everyone criticised the poor bastard for his outrageous taste in colours.

All day he tramped up and down stairs, waiting for hours in waiting rooms, chasing on vain errands and clutching at straws. Net result: nothing.

Poor bastard.

He was so anxious not to waste time or money that he never even stopped for a bite to eat. (Don't feel sorry for him, though. He was quite used to it.)

By six o'clock he had had quite enough and decided to retreat to a little boulevard bar he knew well, which served the best glass of absinthe for miles around. A place where, for four sous, you could get 'a bit of Paradise in your belly', as the late, great Scribe says.* A taste of heaven for all poor bastards. And there he sat, preparing to dip his lips into the sacred liquid, when his eye was caught by a lady at the next table, an unbelievably beautiful and radiant lady who was watching our hero preparing to drown his sorrows with a look of great compassion.

'Poor bastard,' she said, but so gently that it sounded like the music of angels, 'you look rather miserable.'

'Miserable? You can say that again!'

'Perhaps I can help you, then. You see, I happen to be a Good Fairy. Tell me, is there something I can do to make you happy again?'

'There certainly is, Good Fairy. All I need is twenty francs a day for the rest of my life.'

'Well, that's not much to ask for. I can grant your wish here and now, if that's what you really want.'

Twenty francs a day? *Every* day? The poor bastard could hardly believe his luck.

'There's just one thing,' went on the Good Fairy. 'I won't be able to come and bring you your twenty francs every single day, so would you very much mind if I gave you the whole lot in advance? Because of course I also know exactly how long you've got to live.'

The whole lot?

Can you imagine how the poor bastard felt?

Not only was he being guaranteed twenty francs a day for the rest of his life, but he could get his hands on the whole lot *now*!

So the Good Fairy worked out the grand total in her head.

'There you are,' she said. 'It's all yours.'

And she counted out on the table the princely sum of 30 frs. (thirty francs).

A day and a half! He only had another day and a half to live. Poor bastard.

'Well,' he thought, 'it could be a lot worse. Yes, it could be a great deal worse.'

And, feeling much better, he went off to spend it all on riotous living.

* Are you *sure* the late, great Scribe said that? – Ed.

# ANIMAL POWER

You may remember the vigorous campaign I conducted in these columns a while ago to encourage people to stop using coal, oil and other fuels to drive their machinery, and to use animal energy instead.

Well, the idea is catching on.

M. Louis Delmer, an influential engineer from Malines, has already converted many plants and factories to a system of hippo-mobilisation, or what I would simply call horse power. And I hear that the first horse-cycles have had a great success in England.

Meanwhile, M. Adrien de Gerlache, the daring Belgian explorer, is even now preparing for another expedition to the South Pole and has had three bear-boats made for the purpose. These are large propeller-driven skiffs, the power coming from a polar beer exercising in a wheel, rather like the squirrels you sometimes see in cages in France.

So things are beginning to happen, and happen fast.

Because engineers have at last woken up to the fact that the earth's resources are not inexhaustible and that the day will come, sooner than we realise, when our globe, hollowed out inside like an old turnip, will not yield another lump of coal or drop of oil.

And when that happens, how will you drive your steam engines and your motor bicycles then, you idiots, you cretins?

'When that day comes,' I hear you say, 'I'll be long dead and gone, so I don't give a damn what happens.'

Well, so much for logic, not to mention your concern for mankind. Luckily, not everyone is like you. There are a few souls endowed with selflessness, completely without any thought of personal gain, who are quietly working for the generations to come.

And I have recently been privileged to visit a few of the factories now using the systems I have so strenuously advocated. One of them, for instance, is powered by the efforts of 30,000 mice, representing in toto about forty horse-power. The mice are divided into two relays and do shifts of three hours on, three hours off, to drive a huge hollow wheel which keeps turning at an impressive, regular pace. And the energy gained is absolutely free, because the minimal cost of food and bedding (all the straw, crusts, old cheese and domestic scraps come from a nearby town) is more than made up for by the excellent manure produced by the little workers (300 kilos a day, or more than 100,000 kilos a year!).

But the most interesting factory I visited was one driven by frog power. The principle involved was the same as at the mouse-driven factory: a large hollow wheel, not unlike the treadmill used by the English for prisoners condemned to hard labour. (The difference being that we use frogs, whereas they use well-known aesthetes.) No-one who has not seen one at work can have any idea of the thrust produced by a fit male frog when it jumps. This particular wheel is about one-third covered in water and, to prevent the agile little creatures enjoying the pleasures of their native element for too long, has a small electric current passed through it once a minute, which encourages the frogs to rise sharply in unison and apply pressure to the inside of the wheel. (Ever since Galvani carried out his experiments on their Italian forebears, frogs have possessed an immense aversion to electricity.) The energy derived from the 18,000 or so frogs working at present in the factory amounts to no less than sixty horse-power.

A striking proof of the truth of my case.

I will return to this absorbing subject in a later bulletin.


## THE FAILED FIANCÉ

Recently I became engaged to be married (about which more anon) and was suddenly reminded of something which happened to my friend Sapeck years ago. Sapeck was walking down the Boulevard St. Michel one Sunday evening, minding his own business, when he was approached by a Lycée schoolboy who came up cap in hand and asked him very politely:

'Excuse me, sir – I wonder if you would do me a favour?'

'Of course, dear boy,' said Sapeck. 'There is nothing I would rather do. Tell me what it is.'

'It's very simple, really. I would just like you to come with me to the Lycée St. Louis so that you can pretend to be my uncle saying good-bye to me. You see, we are not meant to be out like this without being accompanied by relations.'

'Certainly, certainly.'

So off they went together, Sapeck looking his most grown-up and respectable, and the boy looking rather pleased with himself.

When they got to the school entrance and saw the vice-principal waiting for the return of his charges, Sapeck put on an even more dignified air, insofar as it was possible, and turned to the boy.

'Good night, dear nephew,' he boomed.

'Good night, dear uncle.'

'Now work hard, my boy, and promise me not to get kept in of a Sunday for extra study. You will never come to harm if you obey Tacitus's wise precept: *Laboremus et bene nos conductemus*. For was it not Lucretius who so justly remarked in one of his immortal lines, *Sine labore et bona conducta ad nihil advenimus*? But above all, treat your teachers at all times with the utmost courtesy and respect. Remember, *Maxime pionibus debetur reverentia*.'

The poor lad had become rather uneasy during this impromptu dog Latin lecture from his new uncle, so he ventured another tentative farewell.

'Well, good night, uncle.'

But Sapeck had other ideas, especially having just noticed a rather expensive gold watch and chain draped across the boy's waistcoat.

'What!' he exclaimed. 'Can I believe my eyes? You young wretch, are you taking your *watch* back to school? Has no-one ever told you that in classical Rome there was a man stationed at the entrance to each place of learning whose sole function was to search pupils in case they tried to bring in a water clock or hour glass under their toga, and to take it away if he found one? He was called the *Scholarius Friscator*. As Sallust so truly said: *Chronometrum juvenibus discipulis procurat distractiones*.'

'But, uncle . . .'

'No buts, my boy. Give me your watch.'

The vice-principal came to his support.

'Go on, boy, give your uncle your watch. You won't be needing it here in school.'

The young student was beginning to fear that he had seen his treasured timepiece for the last time when Sapeck, under whose rough exterior ticks a heart of gold, relented.

'Well, never mind, lad. Keep your watch this once. It can be a symbol for you of the way time passes, never to return. *Fugit irreparabile tempus*, eh?'

So when I was engaged to be married recently (about which more in a moment) I thought of this adventure of Sapeck's and was reminded of an almost identical incident in which I was involved. Identical to begin with, anyway.

I, too, was approached by a young boy from the Lycée. It was a Sunday again, though this time at the fair at Neuilly. And my young schoolboy, just like Sapeck's, came up to me cap in hand and said, very civilly:

'Excuse me, sir – I wonder if you would do me a little favour?'

'Certainly, as long as it does not inconvenience me at all,' I said politely.* 'Tell me what it is.'

'Well, sir . . . But first let me introduce you to my girlfriend. The thing is, we are both very much in love and we need some help.'

So saying, he presented me to a funny little brunette with a slight squint.

I don't know how you feel about little brunettes with squints. Personally, I love them.

I gave her a deep and flattering bow.

'Well, you see,' explained the student, 'I desperately want to have her picture on my mantelpiece at home. But my mother would never let me have any girl's picture on my mantelpiece anywhere in the house, so I have to think of a way round her. And what I thought was this: if I had a photograph taken of her with *you*, I could tell my mother that it was a picture of a teacher of mine taken with his young wife. Then she wouldn't mind at all. Well, are you on, sir?'

Deep down I'm not a bad old thing so I said I was and the three of us repaired to a nearby travelling photographer's booth. After a few intensive minutes we emerged the proud possessors of a startlingly life-like reproduction of her and me on a copper plate, tastefully framed, all for a mere 1 fr. 75, and everyone was happy.

Which brings me to my recent engagement (about which more now). I was not only engaged, I was on the very brink of getting married, till one day my ex-future-father-in-law-to-be took me aside and asked, rather stiffly, I thought:

'By the way, is that other business all over now?'

'Business? What other business?'

'You know. Your liaison with the little squinting brunette girl.'

I explored the deepest recess of my memory. Nowhere, on the spur of the moment, could I find any evidence that I had ever been embroiled with a squinting brunette, undersized or otherwise. I told him as much.

'Then how do you explain *that*?' said my almost-father-in-law,

* This tells you all you need to know about Alphonse Allais (Author's note).

brandishing *that* in my face. God knows where he got it from, but it was the very same photograph.

'I can understand a man having a mistress now and then,' he said. 'I am even prepared to overlook the matter if it is discreetly managed. But when he goes out of his way to have publicity photographs taken . . .!'

He seemed unable to finish his little speech, but his gestures indicated amply that his daughter would never be mine.

All for the best, as it turned out. I have since learnt that she drank like a fish.


# MY WORLD RECORD

Dear Puzzled of Nantes.

Thank you for your letter. Yes, you have been correctly informed. I, Alphonse Allais, am the current holder of the one millimetre free style bicycling record. Not just for France, but for the whole of Europe and America. I am told that there is some Australian who claims to have broken my record, but my manager advises me to make no comment until an official statement is forthcoming.

No, of course I don't mind giving you some details about my record-breaking performance.

Firstly, the machine I use is an all-wooden vélocipède built thirty years ago, in 1864, by a blacksmith from Pont L'Evêque who is unfortunately no longer alive. This particular model is now very rare – in fact, the only person I know who still uses one beside myself is Paul de Gaultier de la Hupinière, an elderly book reviewer who lives in Normandy and relies on it to help meet his deadlines. When it was first put into production, Dunlop was still a baby and Michelin had a long way to go to his first communion, which explains why the tyres on my bicycle are solid cast iron. They aren't as flexible as rubber, of course, but they are a good deal more reliable. Put it this way; I take sharp stones in my stride and broken glass doesn't stand a chance against me.

Yes, your friend is quite right. I do indeed hold the world millimetre record on the track as well as on the road. My track record stands at 1/17,000 of a second and was accomplished entirely without the aid of pacemakers. My road record is not quite so good: 1/14,000 of a second or thereabouts. I should add that this time was set up during a violent thunderstorm which gave me a lot of trouble with strong headwinds. I should also add (perhaps I should not, actually) that my trainer and timekeeper were dead drunk at the time.

In the coming season I hope to improve on my two world records and am already busy preparing for a new attempt. I put in fourteen hours' hard training every day, half of it on wet sand, the other half on a bedspread embroidered with a rather impressive picture of a tiger in the jungle.

My diet? I train exclusively on a plain diet of sturgeons' roes from Beluga, washed down with a pure sparkling beverage derived from the grape which comes, I believe, from the Champagne area.

What position in the saddle do I personally recommend? Well, right from the start I have always followed the advice of my grandmother who, when I was still very young, made me learn the following rhyme by heart:—

> As rigid as a cyclamen
> Bestride your bicycle! Amen.

So I never lean forward over the handlebars at all but remain in an absolutely upright position. And there you have as much of my technique as modesty permits and patience allows. For further information, I refer you to my forthcoming book: *Fan de Cycle*.

# A PETITION

Onézime Lahilat, a law-abiding citizen of the town of A-on-B, or even B-on-Sea, was in the habit every weekday morning of walking to the station to buy his daily paper and watch the Paris express go by.

One day, as he was coming back from the station, he was just passing the ironmonger's next to the Café de la Poste when he got involved in a moderately serious accident. A pot came flying out of the shop and broke against his right ankle, showering its contents (greasy juices and organic offal) on the poor man's light chamois-coloured trousers. The main result of this disaster was that a middle-aged woman, who was not only the wife of the ironmonger but also the cause of the accident, burst into loud, ill-mannered laughter. (There was a secondary result; their young lout of an assistant burst into identical laughter, revealing a set of yellow, curiously vulpine teeth.)

Onézime Lahilat felt rather upset, not so much by the accident itself, as by the crude mirth it released in these intellectually deprived people. He carefully mopped the disaster area with his checked handkerchief and murmured:

'I do think you might be a bit more careful.'

At which the ironmonger himself emerged and shouted angrily:

'Careful? You stupid, clumsy oaf! If you don't like people throwing rubbish out on the pavement, all you have to do is cross over and walk on the other side!'

'Which is just what I shall do in future,' said Onézime Lahilat, rather coldly.

And it was just what he did do in future. Heretofore, he had always walked to the station along the right-hand side of the main street and come back via the left-hand side; from now on he took the unconventional course of sticking to the right-hand side both on the way there and on the way back.

But after a while it began to trouble his conscience.

Was a trivial disagreement with a tradesman really enough to justify his abandoning one side of the main street altogether? he wondered. Might not his action perhaps be described as high-handed and selfish? Could he even be failing in his duty as a citizen, voter and tax-payer, if he perpetually discriminated against one side of the public highway?

Eventually his storm-wracked conscience could take it no longer, and he sat down to draft a petition to M. Carnot, the President of the French Republic. He wrote it out on fine white official paper, adopted the most respectful tone and explained everything in great detail. It ended as follows:

'. . . in view of the above-mentioned facts, the signatory of this petition humbly begs the Head of State to authorise him to adhere exclusively to the right-hand side of the main street of B-on-Sea.'

By great good fortune our land of France is governed over by a man of honour, in the shape of M. Carnot, who takes a deep pride in his job and insists on keeping an eye on everything personally, as he so strikingly puts it. (Which is at least much better, let me add, both for the health of our supreme office-holder and for the state of the nation, than having a President who goes off gallivant-

ing in the cafés of Montmartre till two or three in the morning.)
So when M. Carnot came to read the petition from Onézime
Lahilat, a flicker of keen interest passed across his face. He turned
to one of his colleagues.

'What do you think of this, Kornprobst?'

'Well,' said the Minister for the Navy, 'well . . . in this matter I
feel in full agreement with you, M. le Président.'

'I agree. It's a matter for Loubet, not for me.'

M. Kornprobst sounded a gong and a mounted republican
guard appeared.

'For the Ministry of the Interior!' snapped Kornprobst, in the
superior tone of voice which naval officers slip into as soon as they
have a mere military man to deal with.

'And tell Loubet to act sharp,' he added. 'It's important!'

The mounted republican guard dashed off, leaving his horse
behind. (The Ministry of the Interior being only fifty yards off, it
was quicker that way.) Loubet took the petition and studied it.

'M. le Président is very kind,' he murmured, 'but he does sometimes pass on to me things which are not strictly my business at all.
This, of course, is something for the local police chief to deal with.'

He called for some paper and wrote a note to the police chief in
question, asking him as a favour to get the matter settled as soon
as possible.

When the note arrived, the police chief was just settling down
with a very different piece of business (young, brunette, very
pretty).

'For heaven's sake,' he broke off long enough to say, 'what on
earth has this got to do with me! This is the mayor's business, not
mine. Send me a gendarme!'

'Sir,' said a voice.

It was a gendarme. The police chief briefed him.

'And tell the mayor to get the matter expedited.'

(He said 'expedited' just to impress the gendarme.)

When the mayor received the petition, he went as pale as a
ghost.

'What a time for this to come along!' he thought. 'Just as the
New Year's Honours List is being decided.'

By now it was quite late in the day. Everyone who was anyone
in B-on-Sea was just sitting down to dinner. But it never occurred
to the mayor to take the responsibility of the decision himself. He
called for a police sergeant and gave him fifteen notes to bear to
the town councillors, summoning them to a council meeting extra-

ordinary. They all turned up except one who was dead. The mayor explained to them what it was all about and they settled down to a full and frank discussion, which did not end until midnight.

I am privileged to be able to bring to my readers the decision of the council, which was as follows:

'Wheareas, etc. etc. etc. . . . .

'Whereas the considerations adduced by Onézime Lahilat do not seem to be sufficiently well grounded, and such a precedent would be a source of great inconvenience . . . .

'Whereas the municipal authority has provided a pavement on each side of the street so that equal use should be made of both . . . .

'Whereas, if the entire population of B-on-Sea took it into its head to start favouring one side of the main street and ignoring the other, or indeed vice versa . . . .

'Therefore the Town Council of B-on-Sea does *not* permit Onézime Lahilat to make exclusive use of the right-hand pavement of the aforesaid main street.'


# THE HENRI II CHEST

There comes a moment at every dinner party when the conversation becomes almost impossibly liberal, and this dinner party was no exception. Unanimously we decided to inveigh against the horrible and unnatural practice of slavery, the subject having been brought up by a plump young man said to be the illegitimate son of a cardinal. (A rumour based entirely on his rubicund complexion, which was a bright monsignorial scarlet.)

It was a high-spirited gathering, most of those present being Portuguese; as the Arab proverb says, who ever heard of a Portuguese being a wet blanket? According to the notes in my diary, the names of these Portuguese guests were 'Major Saligo, et Timeo Danaos et Dona Ferentes,' (the only lady present) 'et Sinon, et Vero, et Ben Trovato' and several others whom I have forgotten. The only Frenchmen present were the scarlet bastard, a naval officer called Becque-Danlot and myself.

When I said just now that we all inveighed against slavery, I was guilty of a slight exaggeration. Captain Becque-Danlot seemed in no mood for inveighing either against slavery or against anything else. But the fair Dona Ferentes was the only one who noticed his abstention.

'What about you, Captain?' she said in her beautiful Portuguese accent. 'Does that not revolt you, the thought of men being sold by other men in this horrible traffic?'

'Yes, indeed, senhora,' said the Captain. 'It disgusts me more than I can say. But a man who has done what *I* have done would be a hypocrite if he condemned the institution of slavery.'

After a pause, he said dramatically:

'You see – I too have sold a man!'

The Captain did not seem particularly tortured by the memory of his misdeed, for he burst into long and loud laughter at the thought of it.

'*You*, Captain? You, the personification of the honour of the French Navy? You have sold a man?'

'Yes, yes, I really did once sell a man,' said Becque-Danlot, between roars of laughter.

'Was that in Africa?'

'No, not in Africa. Here in France.'

'In France!'

'Better still; here in Paris.'

'Paris!'

'And not just anywhere in Paris. I sold him at the Auction Rooms in the rue Drouot.'

It suddenly occurred to the assembled company that the fearless seamen might be pulling our communal leg. The cardinal's natural son spoke up for all of us.

'May we suggest, Captain, that you go and tell that to the marines?'

The Captain took no notice.

'Yes, senhora, yes, gentlemen, I once put up a man for auction in the rue Drouot and sold him. It wasn't a particularly profitable transaction – I lost 350 francs on the deal, as a matter of fact – but I centainly got my money's worth.'

We all sat mystified.

'Tell us about it,' said Dona Ferentes.

It is well known that a French sailor never refuses an order given by an Andalusian lady. So he obeyed, pausing only for the traditional rituals of lighting a cigar, contemplating the blue spiral of smoke, etc., etc., all of which I shall completely ignore.

\*       \*       \*

It happened about three years ago. I had been out in Senegal and had come back to Paris with six months' leave of absence to convalesce from illness, so as you can imagine I was determined to convalesce in style. Luckily I had just come into a small inheritance which enabled me to rent a ground floor apartment in the rue Brémontier, do it up properly and prepare for six months of non-stop festivity.

Well, one evening I met a young lady in the Jardin-de-Paris whom I took to immediately. I don't say she was particularly pretty, but she had real character and charm, and modesty to match, unlike most of the tarts you find round here.

We got talking and she told me her life story. A damnably tedious life story it was, too – father an Army general, brought up in the barracks, mother dies, father remarries, wicked stepmother, endless scenes, life becomes impossible, runs away from home, despair, considers suicide – till I had to cut the whole recital short, even if she was dabbing at her tears with a scented handkerchief the whole damned time.

I'm sure you can guess the outcome. I took the young lady home with me, let her stay in my place as long as she wanted and even got a treasure of a lady's maid to look after her. I set her up nicely, as you might say. Gave her everything she wanted, treated her right and behaved like a perfect gentleman.

I didn't see much of her during the day, but I always turned up about six in the evening to take her out to a concert, or to a theatre or just to dine.

The tiresome thing was, that she seemed to fall passionately in love with me after a while and took to saying:

'When you have to go away and leave me, my darling, I think I shall kill myself.'

The deuce she would! I was beginning to get rather worried about the serious turn things were taking, when one day the little treasure of a maid gave me a note which she asked me to read later in the morning. I did, and it said:

It's about time someone told Monsieur about Madame's little games, because as soon as Monsieur disappears in the morning Madame lets in a little gigolo as low-class as I've ever seen and he stays here all day, and if Monsieur ever does come back unexpectedly, which did happen once, they have a plan, which is for the gigolo to hide in the big Henri II chest we use for keeping firewood in during the winter.

What your eye doesn't see, her heart doesn't grieve for! The gigolo gentleman is quite comfortable while Monsieur is here because the lid doesn't fit very well and the chest is very big. If Monsieur wants to catch him, the best time is about two in the afternoon.

## Marie

Well, I had never heard such a vile, terrible, unbelievable pack of lies in my life. Despite which I turned up promptly at two o'clock that afternoon and got a few nods and winks from my little treasure as much as to say that my journey had not been in vain. Ellen (I don't think I told you that my mistress was called Ellen) received me with open arms as cool as you like and said with a big smile:

'Dearest! How wonderful to see you out of the blue like this!'

I had a quick look at the chest. Wherever the key was, it wasn't in the keyhole. But it wasn't an easy thing to hide, being a large period cast iron sort of thing and it took only the odd passing intimacy to establish that it was now in my lady friend's pocket. So it was all true, eh!

Where my next idea came from I haven't a notion. I've always liked to think it was a sudden flash of genius, because what I did was send Ellen off to buy a tie for me in a shop a long way away, in the avenue de Villiers, on the pretext that she was the only person whose taste I could trust. Then, as soon as she had gone, I stopped a cab and got the concierge to help me load the chest aboard en route for the auction rooms!

When I arrived I found there was already a sale in progress, but it needed only the judicious greasing of a few palms here and there to make sure my chest was included as a late entry. They didn't particularly like my not being able to produce a key for it but they reckoned that it should be in a good condition inside as it was out, so they accepted it for auction.

And before half an hour had passed, it had been bought by a man from the Auvergne for the princely sum of 250 francs (I had only paid 600 francs for the thing).

I stayed to watch the chest being loaded on to an enormous removal cart where it was quickly submerged beneath an extraordinary flood of other objects – bedsteads, bronze statuettes, crates of wine, bird-cages, child carriages, chandeliers, etc. etc. . . . and, presumably, the gigolo right at the bottom shouting for help through the thick, sound-proof walls of my antique chest.

Where did fate take him next? How soon did he regain his liberty? Or is he still there to this very day? Ah, senhora and gentlemen, these weighty questions have to remain unanswered for the very simple reason that I found it impossible to raise any interest in the answers. All I can tell you is that I never laughed so much in my life as I did that day.

I never did see Ellen again. The little treasure told me that when she came back with the tie she packed her things and left straightaway, without so much as making any comment on the missing item of furniture. Can't say it worried me much. Funny thing is, though, I can't bear large antique chests any more.

# IN WHICH CAPTAIN CAP TAKES GREAT EXCEPTION TO BEING MADE A FOOL OF

Captain Cap pushed a coin into the slot machine and waited. Nothing happened. Not the slightest bar of chocolate. Not even a peanut. He flew into the most tremendous rage and kicked the machine.

'Pack of thieves!' he roared. 'I'll get you for this!'

And added to me, rather more softly:

'I'll come back with a stick of dynamite tonight and blow their damned machine to smithereens.'

'Come on, Cap!' I said. 'That's going a bit far, just to get two sous back.'

'It's not the two sous. I don't give a damn about the two sous. I just don't like being made a fool of.'

I can bear this out, having seen Cap react to similar imagined affronts in the past. When he gets the idea that mankind has conspired to short-change him, nothing less than the most violent and drastic revenge will do. I once saw him weigh out 500 grammes of sugar he had bought from a grocer and find that it came only to 485. The next day he went back to the shop and quietly sprinkled strychnine in their salt, sugar and flour.

'Please don't think I was upset about the 15 grammes they cheated me out of,' he told me apologetically. 'I really didn't mind about that. I just don't like being made a fool of.'

Sometimes he went even further.

I remember once, when he had been staying in an hotel in

Marseille and was packing his bags on the last day, he found that he was missing a collar. There was only one possible explanation. One of the staff must have stolen it while he was out of the room. So the Cap took immediate revenge action. Instead of going back to Paris, where he was wanted on urgent business, he took the next boat to Trieste. As you all know, Trieste, along with Hamburg, is the most important market in Europe for wild animals and zoo specimens, and as soon as Cap arrived he was lucky enough to find a real bargain: a large wild jaguar which was so uncontrollable that no-one wanted him, going dirt cheap. So Cap bought the beast and packed him into a large trunk made, apart from a few air holes, entirely of solid steel, then set sail again with his ferocious travelling companion on a fast boat bound for Marseille.

*          *          *

Naturalists have observed that however savage a jaguar may be in its natural state, it becomes even more unsociable when locked away in a trunk for seven days, even if its owner has taken the precaution of packing twelve kilos of fresh horse meat with it. Captain Cap's jaguar was no exception to this general rule.

Unfortunately, the hotel waiter who had already been guilty of the theft of a collar was unaware of this and took advantage of Cap's return to investigate the possibility of abstracting a handkerchief. Once more, he opened the trunk. But, oh dear, this time the lid rose faster than the delinquent hotel employee could possibly have anticipated . . . .

Properly grateful for deliverance from such cramped quarters, the jaguar celebrated with a little orgy of carnage which involved the demise of the guilty waiter, two chamber maids, three tourists, the manager, the manager's wife and several passing gentlemen of no particular importance.

Yes, when a jaguar is having a good time, it's very hard to stop him.

'And do you know?' twinkles Captain Cap whenever he relates this tale, 'Do you know, I have often been back to that hotel since then, and have never lost so much as a single collar stud? Not that I cared a damn about the collar in the first place. It's just that I hate to be made a fool of.'

# THE BOY AND THE EEL

I have heard our best comic songwriters indulge in the wildest flights of fancy. I have seen playwrights dream up some totally unlikely situations, especially when drunk. But I have never known either of them produce anything half so incredible, so impossible, as the things which happen in everyday life. The sort of thing of which drama critics are wont to say: 'If this were not on the stage but in the papers, no-one would believe it.'

I apologise for this pseudo-philosophical preamble but it is designed to prepare my worthy readers for a little real-life incident. Many of you will greet it with an incredulous smile, garnished no doubt with a shrug of the shoulder and perhaps even topped with a curl of the lip. I don't blame you. The tale I am about to unfold is so fraught with improbability that, did I not know the persons involved intimately, I too would not believe a word of it. As it is, I can vouch for its utter authenticity.

It all started last Friday at about 10.15 a.m. (note the careful circumstantial evidence) when my gardener's wife told her little boy to pop down to the fishmonger's, near the Seine.

'Now listen, Julien,' she said. 'Old Mme Pointu says that they've got some very good eels today, so I want you to get me a nice big one. Here's a five franc piece. Don't pay more than a franc for it, though, and don't let them cheat you with the change.'

Julien was quite used to doing little errands, as his mother had trained him from an early age to go shopping by himself, but he had never been sent to buy a real live eel before so he went off feeling very excited. He ran along throwing the coin up in the air and catching it again, throwing it up and catching it, as boys are wont to do, till – just as he had reached the river – he missed it and saw it roll straight off the quai into the Seine.

Disaster! He dashed to the edge and lay down to look into the river, but it had fallen into at least twenty foot of water and there was no sign of it.

As if things weren't bad enough, a sudden gust of wind then whipped off his beret and a moment later that too was in the water.

Well, he thought, at least he could rescue the beret if he were quick enough. He jumped into a convenient dinghy and rowed out in an effort to save it from a watery grave. He was just in time; when he reached it, the thing was completely waterlogged and about to sink, so he quickly grabbed it and pulled it into the boat. It was then he realised, to his utter amazement, that caught in the beret was an eel, a magnificent eel, which must easily have weighed $1\frac{1}{2}$ lbs.

This unexpected stroke of luck made Julien feel a little better and he went back home bearing the eel for his mother to kill and prepare for cooking.

Which is where the plot thickens.

Because when she cut the eel open, what do you think she found lying in its stomach?

If I told you that she found the five franc piece, would you believe me?

Well, you would be wrong.

There was absolutely no sign of a five franc piece.

For one thing, a long thin creature like an eel could never get a five franc piece down its throat. Even if it could, its stomach is too small to take it.

No, what my gardener's wife found in the eel's stomach was (were) eight 50-centime pieces. Adding up to a total of four francs. Which was exactly the amount of change she had expected to get back from the fishmonger.

Quite a nice little coincidence, don't you think?


## PUTTING THE RECORD STRAIGHT

Many people have been amazed, and rightly so, at the absence of my name from the list of new Cabinet Ministers, and they have demanded to know the truth behind it. Was it an unforgiveable oversight? Or is there some conspiracy to keep me out of office? The first theory is, of course, hardly possible. As for the second, I would rather not comment. I prefer to let France judge for herself. These are the facts, as follows.

On Monday December 5th 1892, at nine o'clock on the dot or perhaps half past nine, my bell was rung by none other than M. Bourgeois, the Foreign Secretary. I jumped into my trousers, pulled on a shirt, hastily pinned on my Académie Française ribbon and opened the door.

'President Carnot has sent for you,' he announced. 'I have a carriage waiting. Let's go.'

'Right – I'll just get dressed properly.'

'No time for that – you look fine just as you are.'

'But my dear Bourgeois, for the President of France . . . .'

M. Bourgeois cut off the rest of the sentence by the simple expedient of grasping me firmly in one hand, hauling me down the four storeys from my bachelor apartment to the ground floor and thrusting me into his cab. Five minutes later we were in the Palais de l'Elysée.

\*    \*    \*

I was received most graciously by President Carnot, who ushered me to a seat without seeming to notice my lack of jacket, my moose-skin slippers or my balmoral (a kind of Scottich headwear).

'Now tell me,' he said, 'which Ministry would you prefer to take over?'

My first instinct was to ask for the Ministry of Arts. As you know, the Minister for the Arts is given automatic entrée to the Paris Conservatoire where there are many beautiful young pupils to hand.

My second instinct was to plump for the Treasury, for reasons I need not explain.

But if there is any instinct more highly developed in me than lust and avarice, it is patriotism. So I made this firm reply:

'M. le Président, I humbly ask to be given the War Office.'

'Ah! Do you have any particular reforms in mind in the field of defence?'

'I'll say!' I replied, a little informally perhaps. But Carnot merely invited me courteously to unfold my plans for progress and improvement.

'Right. First, I shall do away with the entire artillery . . . .'

'!!!'

'Yes, I insist. The noise made by modern cannons and field artillery is quite intolerable, especially if you have the bad luck to live next to a firing range; it must be banned forthwith.'

M. Carnot muttered something which I did not catch.

'I'm afraid the cavalry will also have no place in my plans for the future of the French Army.'

'???'

'I'm sorry, I must insist. The human suffering involved in so many falls from horses and the widespread incidence of so many bruised buttocks is something which no modern army should have on its conscience.'

'I see. Will you spare the infantry?'

'The infantry? Not a chance! Tell me, M. le Président, have you ever served as an ordinary foot soldier?'

For a few moments M. Carnot seemed to be riffling through his memories: then he said firmly: –

'Never.'

'Then you have *no* idea how blistered and footsore the average poor bloody infantryman gets on the average forced march. You have no idea, M. le Président, absolutely no idea at all.'

'Hmm. Will you keep the engineers?'

'I have nothing personal against the engineers, but . . . well, let me tell you a little story. Some years ago I had a little girlfriend from America whose name was Angie, and whom I dearly wished to marry. And she might well have become my wife had she not left me for a friend of mine called Caran d'Ache. Friend! Anyway, this girl, whose full name was Angie Nears, left such a gaping hole in my heart that ever since I only have to hear her name, or one like it, to be overcome by distressing memories. Hence my aversion to the Engineers. Yes, I would do away with them as well.'

I fell silent. The President of France wiped away a furtive tear.

'Which brings us to the catering corps. A fine body of men, M. le Président, but I fail to see any advantage in preserving them as a regiment when, after my reforms, there will be no-one left for them to feed.'

At this point the head of state rose to his feet, as if to indicate that the audience was now over. Having noticed that during the entire session no-one had thought fit to serve drinks, I issued a general invitation to Messrs. Bourgeois and Carnot to come and have a vermouth in the café in the Place Beauvau. Neither of them was, apparently, in a position to accept my offer so I thought it polite not to press them and retired gracefully.

Since then I have not heard a single word from either of them.

# THE IMPRUDENTIAL ASSURANCE
# COMPANY
'To protect you against the risk of penal detention'

(I have received a touching letter from a famous lawyer who wishes to be allowed to make an appeal to our vast and distinguished readership. And why not, I say? They are all yours, my learned colleague.)

As you may know, there was set up in Paris some two years ago a new firm called the 'Compagnie d'Assurances sur le Vol', to enable people to insure themselves against burglary. It has grown and prospered ever since, which I take to be a sure sign that theft is now firmly established as one of our most popular sports.

The principle behind this new institution was most enterprising and I would be disposed to applaud it unreservedly if I did not at the same time find it deplorable that the Company has done so much to protect the victims of burglary and nothing at all to safeguard the interests of those responsible for the burglaries. But surely one cannot have a burgled person without having a burglar? Why, then, should protection be afforded to one and not to the other?

In a perfectly free and equal society (such as we now enjoy) this anomaly, deliberate or not, stands out as a crying injustice. I would go so far as to call it an immoral omission, for it deprives the brave and often heroic burglar of all the honour due to him.

An old judge I know, who has acquired a vast knowledge of the annals of larceny over the years (and thus become doubly dangerous to society), once related to me the exploits of an ex-client of his. They were superb. I can only call them deeds of prowess, passages of arms, feats of single combat – more than enough, at any rate, to make the knights of old look tame indeed. And when one thinks of the long, patient years of study and apprenticeship he had to go through before attaining such perfection, in a society which tends to be hostile to such effort, then one cannot help admiring him and all other unassuming champions of the jemmy and the skeleton key.

For it is no easy trade. His client can sit comfortably at home, assured by his policy and reassured by the police, doing nothing to make the burglar's job any easier – seeking, indeed, to hamper him – while the burglar has not a moment's rest; night and day he is on his lonely beat in country lane and city street. Sometimes, faced with a recalcitrant bourgeois determined to place obstacles in his path, he is even obliged to resort to physical violence. Then the police, cheered on by merciless magistrates, hunt him down implacably. His liberty is perpetually at risk, not to mention his life.

And do you imagine that if, in spite of so many difficulties, he *does* manage to commit an elegantly planned and beautifully executed burglary, he will receive any praise? Far from it. Everyone's sympathy will go the passive object of the burglary, the so-called 'victim'. No-one will spare a word for the burglar. Or if they do, it will not be a very polite word. (Listen to any judge's summing up.)

The injustice involved is so blatant and the loss to their livelihood so grievous that I am astonished that the brotherhood of pickpockets, cut-throats and fellow-swindlers has never gone on strike. A burglar's strike! That would set the cat among the pigeons, indeed. As we all know, 'property is theft'. Ergo, if there were no more theft, there would be no more property. Which would mean no more landlords, no more concierges, no more rent! Can you imagine? Not to mention what chaos there would be in the law courts, with everyone having to be acquitted, all judges having to retire and thousands of unemployed lawyers being set loose to roam the streets. It does not bear thinking about.

There is a very real problem here, therefore, and we must take immediate steps to support the sterling work of all those malefactors without whom our legal and police forces would not have a shred of justification for their existence. And it is for this reason that I propose to found a new insurance company for protection against the risk of imprisonment and to help compensate all those poor wretches condemned by a harsh society to lie in sorrow on a damp prison pallet.

I propose to call the new company the 'Imprudential Assurance Company'. It will have its head office here in Paris, but there will be branches all over France, especially in those parts of the country where the statistics of arrest and detention are highest.

The Company would insure policy holders against every kind of imprisonment including imprisonment for political crimes, though there would be higher premiums for the latter as this branch of crime is becoming increasingly popular. (We would not, however, be prepared to insure anyone appearing before the High Court.)

For a small surcharge, it would be possible to insure against police raids, third degree interrogation, false arrest and other street accidents.

If a client wished to insure himself against the effects of a house search or an appearance before an examining magistrate, there would be a special sliding scale of charges depending both on the intellectual calibre of the magistrate and on the political hue of the customer.

The advantage of insuring one's self against the risk of imprisonment should be obvious not only to professional burglars but to *anyone* liable to sudden arrest, so our scheme will naturally appeal to members of parliament, senators and cabinet ministers as well. And in an age when judicial errors seem to be on the increase, I need hardly say that a policy held with our company will be the only safeguard against total ruin for any innocent man jailed by mistake.

Such, in brief, is the nature of my new enterprise. I appeal to all your readers to lend it the moral and financial support which it deserves. I appeal to them not just for France but for all humanity. I am confident that they will respond to my appeal.


# THE DOGS OF WAR

If the military experts are to be believed, dogs are really going to have their work cut out in the great European wars ahead of us. Apparently there are going to be sentry dogs, reconnaissance dogs, dispatch dogs, anti-bicycle dogs – the way things are going we may not be needing soldiers at all. And I need hardly tell you that the Germans are already ahead of the rest of us in this new-fangled field of military research; not a day goes by without some Prussian officer or other thinking of an ingenious new way of adapting dogs to a military function.

So I think I ought to disclose a highly disturbing development which I had the luck to witness while on holiday recently in the little-known German countryside round Königsberg (little-known to me, at any rate – I was completely lost at the time) because it should be brought to the attention of the relevant authority without delay.

I had just emerged from a large wood in which I had spent a happy morning going round in circles when I was amazed to find myself the witness of the following scene. There before me was a whole company of French and Russian soldiers (yes, Russian soldiers! I couldn't believe my eyes) who were busy . . . .

It might make things simpler if I tell you straightaway that what I saw was a whole company of Germans *dressed up* as French and Russian soldiers. They were busy feeding a large pack of dogs. Or rather, a pack of large dogs, the kind you see in Flanders pulling milk floats. It was most touching. They stroked them and patted them. They talked to them and scratched their ears and called them nauseating pet names. And when it was all over and the dogs were quite full, the false French and pseudo-Russians harnessed them gently to little dog-carts, tethered them to posts and went off, leaving them behind.

But as soon as they had vanished, more soldiers appeared, this time in German uniform, who promptly attacked the dogs brutally, kicking them, whipping them, snatching their bones from them. Then, still shouting furiously at them, they untied them and let them go. Not surprisingly, the poor beasts couldn't wait to get away and set off at top speed cross country in search of their French and Russian friends, dragging the little carts behind them.

What on earth could this amazing demonstration be in aid of? I was baffled. At the same time I had no intention of leaving the area until I had found out, and that very same day I made my way to Königsberg at the risk of being arrested to pursue my patriotic investigations with my usual unshakeable determination and exceptional intelligence. Neither was needed, luckily, as I very soon learned the truth from a rather drunk and indiscreet German lieutenant.

It turned out that the dogs I had seen were being trained to flee from the German army in time of war, and seek refuge with French or Russian soldiers whom they knew to be kind and gentle. The little carts would be loaded with extremely high explosive, capable to killing thousands of men. The charges, moreover, would be set off at exactly the right moment, thanks to a timing device which could be adjusted according to the distance between the German lines and the enemy.

It's as simple as that.

By the way, the dogs have all been made silent by a surgical operation and the wheels of the little carts are made of rubber, so our men will have no inkling of the approach of this deadly mobile war machine.

Soldiers of France, you have been warned!

# ROMANCE IN THE RANKS

It has always been the done thing in the French Army to make fun of the Supply Corps, but the lads in the Supply Corps couldn't care less. Why should they? As they always say, where else in the French Army does everyone get a horse and carriage laid on free and gratis?

Horses and carriages! When young Gaston de Puyrâleux joined up for five years, it was this intoxicating prospect which made him opt for what he took to be the premier branch of the armed forces.

Prior to taking this way out of life's little problems, Gaston had managed to get through two or three legacies which had come his way, none of them lasting much longer than would the contents of a medium-sized watering can in the Sahara Desert at 12.30 p.m. precisely. What with gambling, dud racing tips, pretty girls, high life and low life, young Puyrâleux had been bled white in no time at all.

But he had no regrets, and it was with a high heart that he set off to join the 112th Regiment, the Supply Corps, at Vernon.

Being something of an optimist on the philosophical front, Gaston's motto in life was 'Life is what you make of it', to which he added the admirable rider 'As long as you have fun.' And being an admirable rider himself, he soon quite effortlessly became the finest horseman and driver in the regiment. His prowess was legendary; if he had wanted to, they said, he could easily have got a full supply train through the eye of a needle without touching the sides.

\*       \*       \*

The town of Vernon may be set in the most delightful country, but it is also in its own right a pretty dreary old town. For instance, it is short of women. Oh, of how many women is it short! Women worth calling women, if you follow me.

Which meant that young Gaston was faced with a choice between, on the one hand, going whoring and, on the other hand, going wife-chasing. In such a quandary he had no hesitation. He opted for both.

In quick succession he became the lover both of fixed-price ladies of the street and of impressionable tradeswomen, not to mention the wives of several civil servants and a Fat Lady in a fair.

Let me say straightaway that his passion for the last-named never got beyond the platonic stage, despite which it was also unfortunately responsible for the ruining of his brilliant army career.

*La Belle Ardennaise* was, according to the sign outside her tent, The Finest Woman of the Century. This may or may not have been the case, but she certainly was one of the most massive. On any other woman her ankles would have done a good job as thighs, and her thighs – well, only a chartered surveyor could have done justice to their suggestive contours. She also went about wearing a huge dark red plush dress set off beautifully by a large scarlet toque. The effect, I can assure you, was rare and wonderful.

And like an idiot Gaston went and fell deeply, hopelessly, in love with *La Belle Ardennaise*.

Sadly, the feeling was not mutual. *La Belle Ardennaise* was not a light woman in any sense of the word and all Gaston's lavish attention and the splendour of his full dress uniform were to no avail.

But he was not the kind of man to take such a humiliating reverse lying down. And having ascertained that *La Belle Ardennaise* slept all by herself in a caravan far from the fair owner and his family, he hatched a plan of Biblical simplicity.

One dark night, accompanied only by his faithful groom Plumard, he crept into the fairground. All was silent save for the low growlings of assorted melancholy wild animals. In less time than it takes to write it, he had harnessed to her caravan two fine horses (property of the French government), taken the brakes off, kicked away the chocks from the wheels . . . .

A moment later horses, caravan and Gaston were proceeding at top speed out of the town into the sleeping countryside.

To begin with there was no sign of any reaction from inside the vehicle.

But hardly were they past the last houses when the caravan window flew open and a loud voice was heard, a rough, strident voice used to giving curt orders. The curt order it gave was: 'Halt!'

The horses halted like a shot. And Gaston immediately took on the look of a soldier who is in a very tight spot indeed.

Because the rough, strident voice was a voice he knew very well indeed, belonging as it did to his commanding officer, Baron Leboult de Montmachin.

Gaston quickly pulled himself together and went over to the window, cap in hand.

There was just enough pale starlight for the colonel to recognise him.

'Is that you, Puyrâleux?'

'Yes, sir, it's me, sir.'

'And what exactly are you up to, may I ask?'

'Well, sir, you see, sir, it was like this, I wasn't feeling all that well, a bit of a headache actually, and I thought a nice ride in the country might do me a bit of good, so anyway . . . .'

The ensuing conversation was not much enjoyed by either side, but it did at least give the colonel a moment or two in which to repair his ravaged toilet. It also gave *La Belle Ardennaise* time to say several most unladylike things to Gaston.

'And now, if you *don't* mind, Puyrâleux,' said Colonel Baron Leboult de Montmachin by way of concluding things, 'I would be most grateful if you would take this vehicle back to where you found it and leave it there. I will have another word with you about this incident in the morning.'

Needless to say, no such conversation ever took place. But Gaston was not overly surprised, when the time came, that he had not been considered for promotion.

Which was a pity, because it's not much fun being in Supply if you're not in demand.

# GOD

It was late, but the party was still in full swing.

The later it got, the more flushed the guests became, and noisier, and more amorous.

Imperceptibly, the ladies began to shed a few inhibitions; likewise a few garments. And as their eyes started to close very gently, their lips began to open wider, revealing the pink and pearly treasure buried within.

Nobody's glass stayed full for very long. Or empty either.

Only the popping of corks and peals of girlish laughter could be heard above the wild singing.

When suddenly the monotonous nagging tick tock of the ancient grandfather clock in the dining room stopped, and they heard it go into the furious grinding noise which always presaged the striking of the hour.

It was midnight.

The twelve strokes rang out slow, stern and solemn, with the vaguely reproachful sound that old family clocks always have. We have struck the midnight hour for all your forebears before you, they seem to say, and we shall be doing the same for your grandsons long after you are dead and gone.

Unwittingly the rowdy company grew a little quieter. The girls stopped laughing. But Albéric, the maddest of them all, raised his glass and announced mock-heroically:

'Gentlemen, it is midnight, and time to deny the existence of God. I give you the toast: There is no God!'

Knock, knock, knock.

There was someone at the front door.

But who could it be? There were no more guests expected. The servants had all been given the night off.

Knock, knock, knock.

The door opened and there stood the imposing figure of an old grey-bearded man wearing a long white robe.

'And who may you be?' they all cried.

The old man answered them very simply.

'I am God.'

They all looked at each other in dismay. All except Albéric. Braver than the rest, he came forward and said promptly:

'I hope that doesn't mean you can't come in and have a little drink with us?'

In his infinite kindness God saw fit to accept the invitation and soon everyone was back in party mood again. They drank, they laughed, they shouted through the night until finally the stars dimmed with the advent of dawn. Then at last the party broke up.

When the time came for God to take leave of his hosts, he could be heard quite happily agreeing with everyone that he did not exist.

# A HOUSE OF MYSTERY

When I read daily newspapers I like to skim through them at top speed, but when it comes to a provincial weekly like *Le Petit Bourguignon* I always take it nice and slowly, giving myself time to savour every moment. If I haven't got time to do it properly I put it aside for a moment when I *can* give it my full attention. Which explains how last week I came to be reading a virgin five-year-old copy of *Le Petit Bourguignon*.

And it was while browsing through this otherwise non-controversial organ that I was stopped dead in my tracks by the following sensational item:–

DIJON REGISTRY OFFICE

October 29, 1895

*Today's Births*

Henri Clerc, at 7 rue Chaussier

Lucien-James Ferrand, at 7 rue Chaussier

Lucienne-Jeanne Walter, at 7 rue Chaussier

Alice Poisot, at 7 rue Chaussier

Marcelle-Jeanne-Marguerite Perret, at 11 rue St.-Philibert

In other words, there had been five births on one day in Dijon. And out of those five births, no less than four had taken place in the very same house.

What a superhuman house it must be.

The very kind of house that France so desperately needs at a time when every Frenchman worthy of the name is plunged into gloom over our declining birth-rate.

Now, if only that house in Dijon could manage four births every day, how happy it would make every patriot worthy of the name.

And if every house in France could put on the same performance, why, in twenty-five years' time we would have produced enough fighting men to satisfy every rabid, bloodthirsty chauvinist worthy of the name!

And yet, and yet . . . I could not help feeling a tinge of doubt no bigger than a man's hand.

Why? Why four births in that one house? And only one in the whole of the rest of Dijon?

'There is something wrong somewhere,' I hear you murmur.

You hear me murmur the very same.

I think you know by now I am not the sort of man to leave any boulevard unexplored, so it will come as no surprise to learn that I wrote immediately to a friend who is high up in local government in Dijon, asking him to shed light on the matter.

'If you can spare time' – I wrote – 'I would be grateful to learn by return of post explanation of multiple births on Oct 29, 1895 at 7 rue Chaussier Dijon Côte-d'Or etc.'

The postal services in Dijon are obviously in a bad way at the moment because it was fully a week before I received a reply. But it was worth waiting for. The tale unfolded by my friend was a dramatic story of intrigue and emotion unparalleled in modern times.

No. 7 rue Chaussier, it turns out, is a house divided into flats occupied by four different families who all get on extremely well with one another. Or at least they did get on well with one another until the anonymous letters started arriving, a few years ago. They were the worst possible kind of anonymous letters: nasty, vicious and unprincipled, accusing everyone in the house of the most un-bridled carryings on, sordid affairs and unmentionable crimes. In no time at all the peace of the house was in ruins. And beyond repair, it seemed, because not only did family stop speaking unto family, but wives started threatening divorce actions and husbands began working out the most efficient ways of murdering wives.

I need hardly tell you, dear reader, that there was not a word of truth in any of the scandalous accusations contained in those letters, which had all been written by some foul-minded, sick, perverted etc. . . . .

But no-one bothered to try to put the unfortunate state of affairs right again. No-one, that is, except the bachelor who lived right at the top of the house in the fifth and final flat and who was so distressed by the whole affair (so my friend tells me) that he decided to put things right by himself.

How, though?

Well, he finally came to the conclusion that you could only fight evil by using its own weapons. So he embarked on a *second* series of anonymous letters and wrote screeds of them to everyone in the house, but this time so glowing with kindness, cheerfulness and lack of recrimination that before very long everyone was happily reconciled and back on the best of terms again.

A celebration was clearly called for. Accordingly the bachelor threw a party for the Clercs and Ferrands and Walters and Poisots, a party such as had never been seen in Dijon since the original launching party for the invention of mustard.

And what a feast it was!

The food was fabulous, out of this world.

The wine – well, not only was there nothing but the best, there was as much of it as anyone wanted.

This reunion party, I should add, took place on January 29.

And exactly nine months later, on October 29, 1895, France suddenly found itself four little citizens better off.

\*     \*     \*

STOP PRESS: I have just discovered that I have been the victim of a particularly cruel and heartless practical joke. I regret to have to tell you that No. 7 rue Chaussier is nothing but a common maternity home.

# FREAKS

In the midst of this Universal Exhibition of 1889, I often find my mind slipping back to the Exhibition of 1878. (An example of that curious phenomenon known as the association of ideas, to which my generation is especially prone. To think that ten years' worth of water has flowed under the bridge since then! It's frightening how old one gets between Universal Exhibitions, especially if they happen fairly infrequently.)

I also find my mind slipping back to the girlfriend I had at the time of the 1878 Exhibition, a sweet little brunette with such an innocent face that even the most cynical priest would have unhesitatingly given her Absolution without Confession. (Mistakenly; a night of orgy was child's play for her.)

And I remember her saying to me at table one day:

'Well, what will you be doing at the Exhibition?'

'What were you expecting me to be doing at the Exhibition?'

'Exhibiting.'

'*Exhibiting?* Exhibiting what?'

'Anything.'

'But I haven't invented anything!'

(This was in the days before I had invented my frosted glass aquarium for shy fish.)

'All right, then,' she said, 'just hire a stall and exhibit a freak or monster or prodigy or something.'

'A prodigy? What prodigy? You, perhaps?'

Her face clouded over fast and she said thunderously:

'Me? A *prodigy*?'

Before the rain of blows could fall, I adopted a sunny, conciliatory tone of voice and said quickly:

'Truly a prodigy, my dearest. A prodigy of grace and charm and beauty.'

I wasn't exaggerating, actually. She really was quite a darling, the little bitch. Pretty nose, large mouth (well-furnished), masses of silky hair, and one of those rosy-white complexions which betoken a woman fed on cream. I won't go so far as to say that I would have thrown myself in the Place Pigalle fountains to save her from drowning, but I was tolerably mad about her.

So in the cause of peace I said:

'All right, all right. Just to please you, I will exhibit a prodigy.'

'Can I be on the door?'

'Yes, you can be on the door.'

'If I make a mistake with the change, you won't beat me?'

'Have I ever beaten you?'

'No, but have you ever let me handle your change before . . .?'

I give you this chunk of dialogue only to let you have some idea of the kind of conversation I had to undergo with Eugénie (or Berthe, or whatever her name was).

Eight days later I received delivery from London of a dwarf, a lovely little dwarf. Now, as everyone knows, when English dwarfs really want to be small they can fool the best microscopes, but (and not everyone knows this) when they want to be spiteful then wild Shetland ponies couldn't stop them. I got one of those. He took an instant dislike to me and spent his entire time in Paris devising trials and tribulations with which to afflict me. On opening day, for example, he stood on tip-toe the whole time and stretched himself upwards to such good effect that he didn't look much smaller than you or me.

My friends all pulled my leg and said: 'Some dwarf you've got there!'

I translated their cynical reactions into English for him, but all he said was:

'Not my fault, is it? You can't be on top form every day.'

And then one evening I came home from the office two hours earlier than I usually arrived, and guess who I found in bed with

Clara! (I remember now, she was called Clara.)

Don't try. You'd never guess in a thousand years.

My dwarf! Yes, ladies and gentlemen, Clara was deceiving me with the Lilliputian Londoner!

I flew into a terrible rage.

Luckily for the midget double-crosser, my first reaction was to raise my fists. By the time I had lowered them again to his height, he had gone.

He didn't come back either.

As for Clara, she was still lying in bed convulsed with laughter.

'And what's so damned funny?' I asked her.

'So funny? Oh, come on, what's wrong with you! You great idiot, there's no need to be jealous of an English *dwarf*, for heaven's sake. I was just curious, that's all. And it was fascinating . . . .'

She collapsed into laughter again, then told me a few details. She was right. I had to admit it *was* funny. I relented completely.

I had gone right off dwarfs by this time, though, and as I still had the Exhibition site all paid for but empty, I got hold of a Japanese giant to put in his place.

Do you remember the Japanese Giant of 1878? Mine, all mine.

And let me tell you, he was *very* different from the little English dwarf. Apart from being appreciably taller, he was also kind, willing and *chaste*.

At least, he seemed endowed with these qualities. I say 'seemed' advisedly, because after only a few days I made another earth-shattering discovery.

I turned up unexpectedly at Camille's place one day (Camille, that was her name, I remember now) only to find, strewn all over the floor, discarded Japanese giant's garments. And there in bed with Camille was . . . guess who!

No, don't try. You'd never guess in a thousand years.

The dwarf again!

That little bastard of an English dwarf had disguised himself as a Japanese giant just to sneak back into Camille's bed.

The episode marked the definitive end of my career as the new Barnum and Bailey.

# THE TEMPLARS

I once knew a man who really *was* a man – a man's man, and as tough as they come. I was in the army at the time, stationed down on the Mediterranean, and he was the sergeant of the squadron. Tough? I'm telling you, he could bring the whole damn squadron to a halt just by tightening his knees on his poor horse. Cross my heart. Funny thing was, he might be a bit rough on the parade ground but off duty he was as nice as they come.

What the hell was he called? One of those funny Alsatian names, it was. Damned if I can remember. Wurtz, or Schwartz, or something like that. Yes, Schwartz, I think. Let's call him Schwartz anyway. He came from Neubrisach, I remember that much, or from near Neubrisach.

By God, he was a man and a half, old Schwartz was!

I remember he came to me one Sunday and said: 'Well, what shall we do today?' 'Anything you like, Schwartz, old boy,' I said. The upshot being that we decided to go for a bit of a row. No sooner said than done; we hired a boat, rowed like mad for a while and there we were, out in the open sea. Lovely day for it, it was too, a bit of wind perhaps but not a cloud to be seen anywhere. So we shot along like greased lightning, only too happy to see the coast slip out of sight behind us for once.

One thing about rowing, though, it does make you ravenous, so it wasn't too long before we stopped for a bit to eat. By God, we stuffed ourselves silly! I've never seen a leg of ham get stripped so fast, almost indecent really. And we were so busy eating that we never noticed how the wind was getting up a bit behind our backs and the water starting to chop about in a funny sort of way.

'Christ, look!' said Schwartz suddenly. 'I think we ought to . . .'

Hold on, hold on, I've got the name wrong. It wasn't Schwartz. It was a bit longer than that – something like Schwartzbach. Yes, Schwartzbach sounds more like it.

Anyway, Schwartzbach said: 'Time to think about turning back, lad.'

All very well to say that, but what if it's blowing up half a storm? Before we could do anything about the situation, a fierce gust of wind took our little sail away, a breaker carried one of the oars off, and there we were, at the mercy of the waves. Turn back, I ask you! All that happened was we went faster and faster out to sea, tossing about like a teetotum. There was only one thing we *could* do, and that was take off our coats and shoes in case the worst happened.

By the time dusk fell, it had become a proper hurricane.

Smashing idea it had been to go out for a quiet day on the blue Mediterranean, I don't think.

Then, getting on for midnight, when it had become so dark you couldn't see a blind thing, there was suddenly a great crash! and a nasty sort of tearing, rending noise. We'd run aground.

Yes, but where?

Schwartzbach, or rather Schwartzbacher, because I remember now his name was Schwartzbacher, anyway Schwartzbacher turned out to be quite hot on geography (clever bastards, these Alsatians) and said straightaway:

'Well, sonny boy, we've just hit the island of Rhodes.'

(By the by, could I make a plea to the authorities to put up a few more name plates on Mediterranean islands? They're hell to tell apart in the dark if you're new to the game.)

It was still as black as the ace of spades and we were wetter than two plates of soup, but somehow we managed to clamber up the rocks till we came out on top of the cliffs and had a look round.

Not a light to be seen anywhere.

Bleeding lovely.

'At this rate we'll miss reveille tomorrow morning,' I said, just for something to say, like.

'Tomorrow night and all,' said Schwartzbacher sombrely.

So any rate we started off on a long walk through scrubby little gorse bushes and prickly furzes, just walking along to keep warm really, with not the faintest idea of where we were heading. Till Schwartzbacher suddenly cried out:

'Hey! A light! Over there – see?'

I looked over where he was pointing and sure enough, there was a light. A long way off and a queer sort of light at that, but a light all the same. Not an ordinary light like the light of a house or the glow of a village but . . . well, a queer sort of light.

We set off again, faster this time. And after a long, long while we finally got there.

What it was was a castle set high on the rocks, a big, impressive-looking, solid sort of castle that didn't somehow give the impression of having been built for fun. One of the towers was obviously meant to be a chapel, because the light we'd seen was the chapel candlelight filtering out through great big Gothic stained glass windows. There was singing coming out too, very serious-sounding singing sung by deep men's voices, enough to make your knees all soft and wobbly.

'Right!' said Schwartzbacher. 'In we go!'

'What? Oh . . . all right. How, though?'

'Easy. We just look round till we find an exit.'

Find an exit, he said, when of course what he meant was find an entrance, but still it came to the same thing so I didn't think on the whole it was worth pointing out his mistake which was probably only due to the cold affecting his judgement anyway. So I didn't bother.

There were plenty of entrances all right, but they were all locked solid and there were no bell-pushes or knockers. There might as well have been no bloody entrances at all. But at last we found a low wall that we managed to scramble over, and after that we were in.

'Now,' said Schwartzbacher, 'now we head straight for the kitchens.'

Easier said than done. They didn't seem to have any kitchens. Least, we wandered round and round the endless corridors like rats caught in a maze, and we never smelt the slightest whiff of food. All there was was the occasional bat flying past and brushing against our faces.

Eventually we found ourselves in a huge great hall and suddenly realised that the singing we had heard right at the beginning was much louder, which meant much closer. Sure enough, we had landed up in the room right next door to the chapel.

'Know what?' said Schwartzbacher (or rather Schwartzbachermann, I remember now), 'We're in the castle of the Knights Templar, that's where we are.'

And as he spoke the words, the great iron door to the chapel swung open and flooded us in light, and there they were, before our very eyes, several hundred of them, all kneeling, all with helmets on and all looking bloody big and strong. As we watched, they rose to their feet with a great clanking noise and turned round. That's when they saw us. And when they saw us, they all drew their swords in one motion and advanced on us blades at the ready.

Well, I don't mind admitting that only one thing crossed my mind and that was the possibility of the ground opening up and

swallowing us. But good old Schwartzbachermann never lost his
nerve for a moment. Quick as a flash he rolled up his sleeves, put
up his fists and shouted:

'All right, you Templars, come on and get me! I don't care if
there's a bleeding thousand of you! Durand's the name, fighting's
the . . .'

Ah, *I* remember now! Durand! That was his name! His father
was a tailor from Aubervilliers. Of course – Durand!

He was a man and a half, was Durand. I often wonder what
became of him.


# D'ESPARBÈS'S REVENGE

He was only a country postman, but he could really deliver the
goods.

Every day he turned up with the post on the dot, and as soon as
I saw him coming I would appear at our door with a glass of old
Calvados in exchange for my letters. An unusual arrangement,
perhaps, but I don't remember him ever complaining. And as
soon as we were comfortably ensconced with refreshments we
would always turn to one of the issues of the day for discussion.
Sometimes we chose one of the great issues of the day. Sometimes
we chose the most trivial we could think of. It didn't matter which
we chose, because I knew that D'Esparbès (that was his name)
would always wind up with the same verdict.

'Don't expect me to take sides,' he would say. 'I am completely
electric.'

(I think he meant 'eclectic'.)

There was a perfectly good reason for his electric view of the
world. Along with his other duties he had to deliver various magazines to all the subscribers in the district and he made a point of
browsing through every weekly or monthly before he delivered it.
Which meant that one day he would imbibe socialist dogma, the
next day reactionary ideas, the following day the latest satirical
outbursts and the day after that straight Catholicism. Small
wonder if he had ended up being the most broad-mindest person
possible; not only had he rid himself of any sense of prejudice or
political bias, he had also lost all idealism, all crusading fervour,
all will to change the world. He was, in a word, electric.

But if D'Esparbès's mind was a sea frequented by the floating wrecks of dead political ideas, it was also illuminated by the light of one sublime lighthouse. Love.

D'Esparbès was in love.

He was in love with a widow who lived nearby, a well-built brunette with little side-curls who may not have been quite as young as she used to be but was still every bit as attractive. For her part, the well-built and attractive widow was far from insensible to the charms of D'Esparbès's young limbs (I use the term loosely) and made no secret of her feelings. Thus it came to pass that when our country postman went to deliver the fair widow's mail, he was wont to tarry longer than the mere handing over of a packet of letters might seem to warrant. Ah well, country folk are fairly tolerant in these matters.

But one morning D'Esparbès turned up with my morning papers and post without his usual little opening quip (it was always different from the day's before without ever actually changing very much) and looking as grim as death. All the light had gone out of his eyes; his brow was like thunder.

'You look ghastly, D'Esparbès,' I said sympathetically. 'What seems to be the trouble?'

'Nothing,' he said. 'It's nothing . . . really, it's nothing.'

Luckily, I have this gift for getting people to talk and five minutes later I knew everything there was to know.

It was quite simple. His attractive widow was being unfaithful to him. She had taken another lover on the side.

And who do you think the other lover was?

The local vicar.

L'abbé Chamelle, the curé of Cornouilly.

One of those low-down clergymen who make you wonder if bishops have the faintest idea just what kind of men they send out to look after all those nice respectable country parishes.

A real cad.

Small wonder if D'Esparbès was burning with fury.

'I'll get even with him for this, though!' he told me. 'I'll get my revenge on him, see if I don't!'

And so he did, even if the manner of his revenge makes the ink run cold in my pen as I describe it for you.

One evening our humble postman sallied forth after dinner to Houlbec, to visit one of those public establishments of which there are so many in our small seaside towns, the kind of establishment frequented mostly by merchant seamen, late night fishermen and girls no better than they ought to be – girls, moreover, who may be amply endowed with physical charms but who are invariably ignorant of the basic rules of hygiene and disease prevention.

D'Esparbès spent a few minutes closeted with one of them (not a merchant seaman or a fisherman – a girl).

And emerged highly satisfied. In all respects. Because shortly afterwards he visited his doctor and received authorisation to stay off work for a full week in order to recover from infection.

Next Sunday, very early, I was awoken by D'Esparbès in person, looking more cheerful than I had ever seen him.

'Game for a bit of fun?' he wanted to know.

I indicated that I was.

'Right! Get your carriage out and come with me to Cornouilly. We're both going to Holy Communion. And I can promise it will be worth it!'

We arrived at Cornouilly just as the congregation was gathering for the said service in the aforesaid church. And as the service got under way, I could tell that the poor Abbé Chamelle was not putting much effort into the aforesaid sacred proceedings. Truth to tell, he looked pretty sickly and seemed to find it quite a job just getting up the altar steps.

D'Esparbès, meanwhile, was killing himself with silent laughter.

Eventually the time came for the priest to present the chalice full of the blood of Christ to his flock, then to take a sip himself of the very same cheap Graves (1 fr. 80 a cask, wholesale). And it was at that moment that D'Esparbès stood up in his pew and shouted out, a bit sarcastically, I thought:

'Watch it, padre! No alcohol with your complaint! Doctor's orders!'


# ARFLED

I may be rich and famous now, but five or six years ago things were very different. (May I take this opportunity, by the way, of denying the widespread rumour that my meteoric rise was due entirely to my hypnotic effect on influential women? Alas, I had to rely solely on talent.)

If you had met me in those days you would never have guessed that I was about to rocket to fame. You would have found my

means modest, my habits humble, my *modi operandi* not always
moral, my possessions paltry and my credit chimerical. To be more
precise, I was living in a guest house called the 'Hôtel des Trois
Hémisphères' in the rue des Victimes, where the clientele apart
from me formed a cross-section of circus and music-hall people
from all over the world. There I rubbed shoulders with contor-
tionists from Chicago, tenors from Toulouse, clowns from Dublin
and even at one point a lady snake-charmer all the way from
Fontainebleau.

It was a very happy house, thanks to the manageress – she was a
wonderful woman and we all loved her. A splendid blonde, just a
touch past her prime perhaps and tending to plumpness, but still
with lovely sparkling eyes and a great sense of fun.

The manager was otherwise. We didn't love him at all. I hated
him. And Arfled *loathed* him.

Arfled? You don't remember Arfled? He was the clown in Fer-
nando's Circus. Arfled was an English lad: very handsome, very
athletic and a fine figure of a man. He could hardly speak French
to save his life, mark you, but when you're as great a mime as
Arfled was it doesn't really seem to matter.

'Arfled is a funny sort of name,' I said to him one day. 'How
did you get it?'

He told me that originally he had been called Alfred but that
the very first time he had had a costume specially made to display
his name the seamstress had muddled the letters up and it had
come out as ARFLED. The new name had appealed to him and
he took to it immediately.

Which is more than you could say for M. Pionce, the manager
of the hotel, whom he detested. Why? Difficult to say, really. My
own theory is that he had actually had a great deal of affection for
the Pionce household as a whole, but that by some quirk of fate it
had all become focussed on Mme Pionce, with none left for Monsieur. Well, it showed he had good taste.

It meant, too, that he provided the two high spots in Mme
Pionce's daily routine. The first came when he left his key at the
desk on the way out in the morning. If he should happen to spy
from the top of the stairs that Mme Pionce was on duty all by
herself, he would descend in radiance. His face would light up
blissfully, his eyes be bathed in sunshine and his mouth take on an
exaggerated Cupid's bow shape, as if the air was filled with divine
sounds and smells. Rapturously he would float down the stairs and
shower compliments on her as best he could.

'Bon joor, Madam Pyonce, commong portay voo? Havay voo passay la bon nooee? Voos etes ploo jolee que jamay. Bon joor madam et bon appetay!'

But if he saw M. Pionce there when he came down, Arfled would immediately turn up his coat collar, pull his hat down over his eyes and change into a dangerous animal, slinking past the desk with a growl in his throat for all the world like a savage guard dog.

Her second high spot came when Arfled returned in the evening, and the same performance (depending on whether M. Pionce was there or not) took place again, all done with such masterly skill that Mme Pionce only had to see Arfled to burst into uncontrollable laughter.

\* \* \*

One morning, when Arfled came down, he found Mme Pionce talking to one of the other guests.

'Is your husband any better today?' he heard the man ask.

'Not really,' she said. 'I'm afraid I shall have to send for the doctor.'

At this, Arfled's face crumbled into a mosaic of despair.

'Monseeor Pyonce ay malade?'

'I'm afraid so, M. Arfled. He has been coughing all night.'

'Toot la nooee? Oh! Oh! Pover omme!'

As soon as he came back in the evening Arfled inquired after M. Pionce's health with the most touching solicitude.

'He seems a bit better, thank you.'

Arfled clasped his hands together, raised his eyes to heaven and went into a paroxysm of gratefulness.

'Mersee, mon Dioo, mersee!'

But this improvement in M. Pionce's health was not maintained. Sadly, he was worse the next day and the doctor ordered him back to bed.

The effect on Arfled was dreadful to behold.

But that evening M. Pionce was slightly better again.

It was enough to bring Arfled to his knees in front of the reception desk, where he improvised a short psalm of thanks.

'Thanks be to thee, O Lord, thanks!!'

Mme Pionce's natural concern for her husband's state of health was never quite strong enough to resist Arfled's little pantomimes, and every time he reacted to the latest news, whether it was good or bad, she simply melted into laughter. So it continued for a week, with M. Pionce alternately improving and deteriorating, Arfled improvising accordingly and Mme Pionce screaming with laughter the whole time.

One evening, though, Arfled came back to find her at the desk surrounded by a small crowd of friends and comforters. From her reddened eyes and drawn features, it was quite clear that things had taken a turn for the worse and that M. Pionce must be in a bad way. But when she saw Arfled and suddenly thought of the way he would react to her latest news, she could not help bursting into peals of laughter and collapsing into her chair. After a minute or two she pulled herself together sufficiently to tell him, between outbursts of helpless hilarity:

'He's . . . he's . . . dead!'


## PATRIOTISM ON THE CHEAP
### An open letter to Paul Déroulède

My dear Paul,

I hope you won't mind my addressing you as 'my dear Paul' even if I have never had the honour of being introduced to you (any more than you have had the honour of being introduced to me)?

Good. Then I shall come to the point straightaway.

Please believe me, my dear Paul, when I say that I, like you, can hardly wait to see the French and Germans at each other's throats. It is my dearest dream to see them busy eviscerating and slaughtering each other, as is only fitting to the national dignity of two great neighbouring peoples.

The only reservation I have about all-out war is its incredible expense.

People simply have no idea how many billions we have spent in the last twenty-five years on feeding, equipping and arming our fighting men, building barracks for them, fortifying our strong-holds, manufacturing powder, smokeless and otherwise . . . .

Why, only the other day I was in Toulouse and with my own eyes I saw a French Navy gun which cost us the modest sum of 1,800 francs (*eighteen hundred francs!*) every time it was fired. If the French people are happy to pay out that kind of money, they must be even worse suckers than I thought.

Ah, my dear Paul, may I confide in you and reveal that I am deeply distressed by the thought of such extravagance?

Poor France! I would dearly love to see her victorious in war. But I would like to see her stay solvent as well.

\*     \*     \*

Which is why it occurs to me that perhaps we could use modern science to help us wage war more economically. In other words, why use gunpowder, which costs a bomb, when we could use *microbes* for nothing?

An intelligent man like you will have caught my drift already. We could easily disband the army, turn the drill-halls into music-halls, sell the cannons as scrap metal – wind up the whole bang shoot, in fact. Instead of supporting such a ridiculously costly (and noisy) set-up, we would merely have to instal a few discreet little laboratories where we would produce the most virulent and pestilential microbes in the best conditions possible.

And then! ... When Germany finally went too far, we wouldn't need to declare war on them. We could simply declare cholera, or smallpox, or all known diseases at the same time. We would hit 'em in the colon: aim for the stomach exclamation mark! and bring the nation to a full stop. (The Ministry of War, I need hardly say, would be replaced by the Ministry of Contagious and Infectious Diseases.) And it would be so easy. Our agents would simply have to infiltrate the nation we all hate so much and leave their little test tubes in the right strategic places . . . .

The great advantage of this kind of offensive, my dear Paul, is that it affects every class of society, individuals of every age, people of all sexes.

Old-fashioned war was all very well in its own way, but it was sadly limited when you consider that it only accounted for able-bodied men between the ages of twenty and forty-five. Do you really want us to restrict ourselves to the slaughter of young German males? You are a strange kind of patriot if you do.

*I* hate the Germans, but I hate all of them – all, all, all!

I hate eight-year-old Bavarian girls. I hate Pomeranian centenarians. I hate old ladies in Frankfurt-am-Main and street urchins in Königsberg!

And with my system we would kill the lot.

What a beautiful vision!

We would get our conquered lands back at last, too. After my bacteria had done their job there might not be anyone left alive there, but what does that matter?

The main thing is that revenge would be ours at last!!

What a nice little chat we've had, my dear Paul. Look after yourself and God bless.


# FINIS BRITANNIAE

I'm afraid our English friends have not had a very good press of late. Their Jubilee celebrations were so ostentatious and arrogant that most of Europe felt distinctly alienated; some of the comments in the Continental press had to be read to be believed.

The loudest voices in this chorus of resentment came, of course, from Germany where they have never been slow to make fun of the British colossus, which they see merely as a huge inflated balloon waiting for the first pin to come along and deflate it.

Well, our friends in Germany speak truer than they know, because their little joke is about to become very prophetic indeed. I now take great pleasure in revealing exclusively that England is on the point of disappearing.

One or two experts have suspected it all along.

'It can't be very long now,' they have told each other over the years.

And now the time has come. The English have taken so much coal and ore and mineral wealth from the bowels of the earth that their country has become light enough to float.

*Yes, the whole island has now been afloat for the past two days.*

It may not be tossing around like a champagne cork* exactly, but it is definitely floating.

I happened to be at Greenwich Observatory on Thursday, and the place was in a state of near-panic. I managed to get an interview with one of the senior astronomers there, the Hon. Sir Loin of Wildhog, and his pessimism was plain for all to see.

'It's true. We have now started moving,' he told me. 'The island is not actually pitching and yawing yet, but this morning the whole of the British Isles moved half a degree to the west. We measured it.'

'My God!' I said.

---

* From a bottle of Léon Laurent, preferably.

'And at our present rate of progress we shall reach America before the end of the year. Always assuming . . .'

'Yes?'

'Always assuming we manage to keep afloat that long,' he said, with the utmost gravity, not to say sense of doom.

I clasped his rough, weather-beaten hand in mine and said: 'God Save the Queen!'

At which Sir Loin could scarce forbear to shed a single tear. And for a moment, my friends, I cannot deny that I felt sorry for old England.

## FINIS BRITANNIAE (CONTINUED)

I recently reported in these pages the imminent disappearance of England, or at least her departure for other climes.

'England is now afloat!' I announced – and not without a tinge of satisfaction, because although I have encountered many Englishmen who were charming as individuals, my feelings as a whole for perfidious, hypocritical and predatory Albion are far from flattering.

But I never thought this bit of news would bring such an impressive response from my brilliant readership – certainly not the avalanche of letters and every other form of communication imaginable which I received.

\*          \*          \*

Among them a telegram from Sir Loin of Wildhog protesting indignantly against the pessimistic remarks which I put into his mouth.

Very sorry to be a cause of distress to such a great gentleman, but I did nothing except transcribe and publish the noble cosmographer's exact words.

And I had a witness in the shape of M. Taupin Blackburn, the negro astronomer, who was present throughout our conversation in Greenwich Park.

\*          \*          \*

I would like to leave the final word on the subject to M. Eugène Foreau, our distinguished scientific colleague, who has sent me a substantial letter packed with irrefutable evidence and brilliant insights.

Here is the crucial passage.

'You are right, my dear Allais, in your assumption that England is now floating like an empty cask after being gutted of her coal and mineral ore.

'Where you are wrong is in claiming that she is also on the move. England may be afloat, but she is not moving for the simple reason that she is *moored in position*.

'No, don't argue: it is a scientifically verifiable proposition. Here, briefly, are the facts.

'English scientists had already become aware of what was likely to happen to their island home at least fifty years ago.

'They considered several different solutions to the problem at the time.

'Some of them were in favour of a "water ballast" system, in other words of weighing the island down by filling the hollowed out spaces in their coal mines with sea water.

'They eventually decided against this method for all sorts of reasons which it would take too long to go into here and now.

'Finally they voted unanimously for another proposed system and a few months later, using telegraphic communications as a pretext, began to secure England to Calais, Ostend, Copenhagen, Ireland etc., by means of strong metal cables under the sea.

'Later they added more cables in order to link the vast floating buoy we call Great Britain to America, China, Australia and so on.

'Practical as ever, the English had contrived to ensure the safety of their native sod without incurring a penny's expense, simply by getting every other country in the world to share the costs.'

## FINAL THOUGHTS ON THE FLOATING OF ENGLAND

I had made up my mind not to return to the subject of England being afloat, thrilling though it is.

But my readers have decided differently and I have been deluged with thousands of letters relative to this bizarre occurrence.

So, as your curiosity is obviously insatiable on this score, I shall relent to the extent of passing on the fascinating points raised by M. Jules Domergue, an economist whose authority nobody, I trust, would seek to dispute.

Here is what he has to say:

'My dear Allais,

'There is no disputing the fact that England is now floating. I experienced it first-hand during my last trip there; as soon as I set foot on dry land at Dover I could feel the ground giving way under me, as if I were passing from a small vessel to a very large one.

'And you are quite right to point out that if England is not yet actually drifting out to sea it is only because she has taken the precaution of mooring herself to various continents by means of so-called telegraphic cables.

'What you have *not* pointed out, and it is your clear duty to do so, is the action that England is bound to take in a forthcoming war (against France for example, and we all know it cannot be long now). Because the day war starts England will simply cut her mooring ropes and use her entire navy as tugs to take the country off to nobody knows where.

'How *could* anyone know? All communications will be completely severed.

'With the result that when we arrive with our invasion force there will be nothing left to invade, except perhaps a large hole like the Maelstrom which our fleet will promptly tumble into.

'Which will make the Admiralty look very silly.

'And will not much impress the rest of Europe, to say nothing of our great allies the Russians.

'It needs working out.

'I can only see one solution, personally. Before we ever declare war on Britain we must destroy all their ships in advance.

'Then we shall be free to go in and take over the British Isles which are, after all, not without their own intrinsic value.

'As long as we don't make the mistake of leaving them where they are. We in turn must attach our ships to the island and bring it across into our waters where we can fix it for instance to Penmarch Point, or off Saint-Jean-de-Luz (there's plenty of room – I've checked). Then we could develop it as a new colony which would be much easier to exploit than Madagascar or that damned nuisance Indo-China.

'Well, my dear Allais, that's the way I see it. What do you think?'

\*       \*       \*

What do I think, my dear Jules? I think it's a splendid idea, and I urge the French nation to take all steps to carry out the plan so that we can at last take our rightful place again as top country.

## CRISIS TIME FOR ENGLAND

I have just received the latest number of the *Kent Messenger*. It contains a story which I know will bring great joy to all those among my brilliant and warm-hearted readership who suffer from Anglophobia.

Here it is.

As follows.

'The last church in Dunwich has just been swallowed up by the sea. Although Dunwich was once a flourishing town containing no less than 20,000 inhabitants and at least six fine churches, the sea has gradually encroached until now the last remaining church has crumbled and vanished into the waves. Soon there will be nothing left of Dunwich but memories and old sea stories.'

Alas, poor Dunwich!

But back to the fascinating *Kent Messenger*.

'Recently we reported that a French humorist, a certain Alphonse Allais, had told his readers that England has started to float. He claimed that so much coal had been taken from underground that our island had become buoyant and was only being kept in position by the underwater telegraph cables we had cleverly used to moor ourselves to other continents.

'Well, it was a good joke.

'Unfortunately, the truth is even more serious than that, and it looks as though the time is not far off when we shall all say: "Farewell England!" Because our coastline is becoming subject to a highly ominous and alarming process, namely the gradual erosion of the land by the sea.

'Nowhere is this more marked than in the counties of Norfolk, Suffolk, Kent and the whole of Yorkshire, adding up to several miles of threatened coastline. The Goodwin Sands were once part of the mainland; now they are six miles out to sea. And in parts of Norfolk things are almost in a state of general retreat – some villages, like Shipden, Eccles, Wimpwell, etc., have completely disappeared over the last few years and the town of Cromer has been forced to move three miles inland, lock, stock and barrel. Other towns under imminent threat of invasion by the sea are Winchelsea, Rye, Sandwich, Southport, Overstrand, Sheringham, Sidestrand, Southwold, Auburn and Halburn.

'Over on the west coast of Britain things are not quite so alarming, but there is no cause for complacency, as even there erosion sometimes reaches a rate of five feet a year.'

And the *Kent Messenger* concludes with this philosophical thought.

'It would be nothing less than tragic if the sea, which has proved England's natural defence for so long, turned out to be our mortal enemy and eventually destroyed us.'

\*       \*       \*

As none of us will probably live to see that happy day, let us at least echo the poet's words:

> On n'en finira donc jamais
> Avec ces N . . . de D . . . d'Angliches!
> Faudrait qu'on les extermin'rait
> Et qu'on les réduise en sandwiches!
> etc., etc., etc., . . .

# IT'S LOVE THAT MAKES YOU GO
# ROUND THE WORLD

He was an officer in the Scottish Navy. His name was Captain MacNee but to his fellow officers he was always Captain Steelcock. He was, in fact, what you might call a man's man. A lady's man, rather. Either way, he was all man. He stood fully six foot two in his stockinged feet, which is the nearest the English can get to saying that he was almost two metres tall. Quite a man.

He was also an immaculate dresser and without doubt the coolest thing in naval uniform since Nelson's Column. (Except when pursuing women, which was his main purpose in life.) To top it all, he was one of the very few officers in the Scottish Navy who insisted on wearing a monocle at all times – the crew of the *Topsy Turvy*, the three-masted frigate over which he assumed total com-

mand next to God, swore that he went to bed with his monocle
still firmly screwed in, though none of them had ever actually seen
him do so.

Nor, come to that, had any of them ever seen him become in
the slightest way involved in the running of the ship. He always
kept implacably aloof from naval matters, whatever the weather,
staying well apart on the bridge. There he strolled up and down
by himself, impeccably dressed, hands behind his back, for all the
world like a gentleman of Edinburgh taking the air in Princes
Street. The running and steering of the ship was left to the first
officer, an old sea-dog from Dundee who knew the sea better than
the back of his hand. Occasionally he came to tell the captain
what course they were on and Steelcock would try to look tremen-
dously interested, but you could see that his mind was far away
and that he really couldn't care less what longitude or latitude
they were in.

His mind was far away, did I say? It was in another world.
Because what Steelcock was doing was thinking about women.
Thinking about the women he had just left. The women he had
still not met. The women he had known and the women he wanted
to know. Just thinking about women, in fact.

Sometimes he would lean on the taffrail for hours, staring out to
sea. Was it because the ocean seemed to him the perfect symbol of
the fickleness of woman? Or was he hoping against hope that a
lovely mermaid would emerge before his eyes? (Personally, I tend
to the first theory. I agree wholeheartedly with the poet when he
says that waves are a symbol of the treachery and duplicity of
women. Be damned to women, say I!)*

But whenever the next port of call came in sight, Steelcock
changed utterly. From being an ordinary man he turned into a
whirlpool of passion, an internal hurricane of longing and lust that
made the worst storm at sea seem mild by comparison. And no
sooner had the ship come alongside the quay than Steelcock leapt
on to land on his way to town, leaving the first officer to deal with
the customs and the ship's brokers. Not, I hasten to add, that
Steelcock was the kind of man to leap like a beast of prey on the
first bit of hireable female flesh he saw (and I am sorry to say that
there are all too many in the average commercial port). No, no.

---

* At the time of writing that paragraph I was convinced that my beloved was in
another man's arms. Now (10.40 p.m.) I can vouch that she is not, so I am very
happy to withdraw such discourteous sentiments.

Steelcock may well have been mad about women, but he liked women to be mad about him as well. Not that he often had far to look; with a passion like his, it was not hard to find women who responded to it. He had violent affairs the way other men have bad colds. In any case, his monocle always had a devastating effect on ladies in British colonies and similar backwaters.

But one day he passed from the sublime to the ridiculous by taking an oath that from now on he would make women not only love him, but *love him and no-one else*. It may have had something to do with the fact he was at St. Pierre in Martinique and had just been introduced to the most delicious Creole girl he had ever come across in his life. How on earth could I possibly describe her? Shall I tear a feather from one of God's angels, dip it in the blue of the sky and try to enumerate her heavenly charms? Not if it means getting more angry letters from anti-vivisectionist readers, so let me simply say that the good Captain shortly found himself in ecstasy (a delightful little spot) for a short season.

Sadly, all good things come to an end, much faster than bad things (life is so badly arranged), and the day came for Captain Steelcock to re-embark and continue his voyage. But for once he could not bear to tear himself away from his new-found love. The *Topsy Turvy*'s anchor was already raised. Her sails were set. Without a captain, though, she had to stay where she was and wait.

At long last, Captain Steelcock managed to break free of the spell. Giving his Creole girl a magnificent farewell kiss, he pressed a quantity of pounds sterling into her hand with a heartfelt apology for not having had time to find a more discreet parting present. The young lady counted the money quickly and put it away looking a little dissatisfied.

'Why so unhappy, my love?' said the captain, somewhat disconcerted. 'Do you feel I have not been generous enough?'

His brown goddess looked up at him and said sweetly;

'Not at all. You have been the perfect gentleman. I only wish your First Officer had been half as generous as you.'

His First Officer! This revelation came as a bolt of lightning to the Captain. Suddenly, a veil was rent, his eyes were opened and he saw women as they really are. And from then on he decided never to worry about love again but to concentrate exclusively on more important matters, such as hygiene and convenience. Wherever he landed henceforth he went straight to the professionals just as you or I might make for the best local pork butcher or greengrocer. And he had no reason to regret it.

Not long ago his ship had to put in at the Camom Isles, a small colony in the Pacific belonging to Luxembourg and famous throughout the Far East for its beautiful climate, not to mention its easy-going way of life. No sooner was he on dry land than Steelcock started looked for a good address at which to sample the latter. He found not one but dozens, simply by being directed to a splendid avenue on the edge of town lined with elegant villas sporting such enticing names as Welcome House, Good Luck Home, Eden Villa and Pavillon Bonne Franquette.

Having always had a weakness for Frenchwomen, Steelcock made a beeline for the last-named where he was received by a lady who had seen earlier (and better) days in Bordeaux, and who introduced him to her tenants, all of them without exception charming and lively girls. Steelcock's eye was caught by a dark beauty from Toulon who seemed to him absolutely perfect, except perhaps that she seemed unacquainted with the finer points of the art of hair-combing, but otherwise perfect, so the happy couple promptly retired together for the night and how they occupied themselves thereafter is none of our business.

But early the next morning the Camom Isles were devastated by an earthquake (see the local paper of the time for full details) so violent that no house remained unscathed, not even the Pavillon Bonne Franquette. The ladies managed to escape, fleeing in what, in any other profession, might have seemed a somewhat scanty uniform, and gathered outside for a hasty rollcall.

There were only two missing – Captain Steelcock and his young companion.

The girls were just coming to the reluctant conclusion that both of them must have perished in the disaster when who should emerge from the wreckage but the captain himself, covered in debris, yet still quite imperturbably wearing his monocle.

'Madame!' he cried to the good lady of Bordeaux. 'Madame, send me another girl, would you? Mine is dead.'

# KEEPING UP APPEARANCES

Like everyone else I have been responsible for a few violent deaths in my time, quite a few in fact. Yes, when I think of all those innocent victims my flesh creeps in a very modest sort of way and my open, friendly face goes a little pale.

Women, mostly.

Ah, when I think of all the poor women who have died for my sake . . . .

Some of them have succumbed to a fatal passion for my irresistible good looks. Others I have simply beaten to death.

One of them had rather better luck than the others. She threw herself in despair from a fifth floor window, and had the great good fortune to land on a greenhouse on her, how shall I say? . . . on her big end. With the happy result that she emerged from her little adventure none the worse for wear, except for multiple lacerations to her . . . big end.

To this day I can remember the anxious young patient turning to the doctor as he dressed her injuries and asking: 'Please tell me, doctor, will it *show*?' To which he replied, rather wittily I thought:

'My dear young lady, that rather depends on you.'

The most recent case in this tragic series of female martyrs to my cause (and a lump comes to my pen as I write these words) was my last lady friend, a certain Miss L . . . N . . . . She was beautiful, but it was the fatal kind of beauty that inspired men to fight over her, and it led to her undoing.

Alas, poor L . . . N . . . of Troyes.

As far as male victims are concerned, I have at least half a dozen premature passings away on my conscience, not counting all those relations of mine who have been driven to an early grave at the sight of my headlong turpitude.

For (and you will find this hard to believe) I have not always been the industrious, sober, plump little bourgeois you see before you today.

No, there was a time when – rue the day! – the author of these lines was a nasty, idle, frivolous student who fled his lectures and spent all his (my) time on the sunny café terraces of the rue de

Médicis, interested only in devising new ways of maddening my (his) contemporaries.

Shameful days, indeed.

Not that my little schemes were always successful. Once, I remember, I took a sincere dislike to a bad-tempered old gentleman who lived on the first floor of the house in which at that time I occupied the penthouse attic. The old gent returned the sentiment wholeheartedly, but obviously felt that at his age and in his circumstances it was beneath him to do anything about the thousand little torments I inflicted on his daily life.

One day I arrived at college – *rara avis* – to take an examination.

And who do you think was one of the examiners?

Correct. The bad-tempered old gentleman, who had come along specially to plumb the depths of my knowledge of botany.

He hadn't far to sink.

He pushed a nutritious vegetable in my direction and said, without any trace of wit or refinement:

'What's that?'

'That, monsieur, is what is known in French as a "choufleur".'

'And in Latin?'

'That I cannot tell you, monsieur. I *can* tell you, though, that the English call it a "cauliflower".'

'Your command of English fails to interest me. Tell me, by what botanical features do you recognise the plant?'

'Monsieur, I can identify a cauliflower without the help of botanical features, thank you very much.'

'Thank *you* very much. That will be all.'

The bad-tempered old gentleman had his revenge by ensuring that I returned to take the exam another time.

But I remember one incident which took a rather more tragic turn.

In those days the Latin Quarter was still full of quaint little old corners, most of which have since fallen beneath the demolisher's pick-axe, and it was quite common to find houses lying lower than their own street so that you could look straight from the pavement into a third floor window. I happened to know a law student who lived in a house like that, a very shy, retiring young lad whose upstairs apartment was exactly the same height as the street outside. If you stood outside, you could look into his front room and feel just as if you were in there with him.

One day, I was walking down his street.

There he was, working away by the window.

I stopped and leant on the balustrade outside, to stare in at him, just as you might gaze at an animal in the Zoo.

A passer-by came over to see what I was staring at, and stayed to gaze with me. Then another one joined us, then two more, then four more, then twenty.

Within a few minutes the audience had grown to a huge crowd, without the student once raising his eyes from his books.

But at last he looked up and saw the throng. And as soon as he realised that he was the centre of attention, he became unutterably confused.

Sadly, the poor boy was quite unable to deal with those thousand silent eyes trained on him, and he lost his head entirely.

Because the only thing he could think of, to keep up appearances in such extraordinary circumstances, was to fetch a rope and hang himself.

# VIRTUE REWARDED

Her name was Clémence. She was young, and soft, and pretty. It would not be true to say that she didn't have a single idea in her pretty little head, either, because one fine sunny morning she *did* have an idea in her pretty little head. She confided it to her boy-friend.

'Let's go out into the country!'

'The country?' said her atrocious boyfriend, whose name was Lemuffle, and that was about the only nice thing you could say about him. 'What the hell would we do in the country?'

'I don't know . . . go for a walk?'

'Whereabouts in the country?'

'Anywhere, I don't mind . . . Bougival, perhaps.'

'What's so bloody special about Bougival?'

'Don't you remember? That's where we first met.'

'So it was. I wish I'd stayed at home now.'

'Oh, you brute! . . . Well, do you want to go to Bougival or don't you?'

'No. We'll go to Joinville.'

'All right, let's go to Joinville.'

'And I'll ask Pignouf if he wants to come with us.'

'Oh, no! Do we really have to take him along?'

'Yes, we do. I don't want to have to listen to *you* all day long. At least Pignouf is fun to be with.'

'All right then, my darling. We'll ask Pignouf along.'

Pignouf, Lemuffle's best friend, was like all best friends – badly brought up, noisy, disloyal behind your back but, you had to admit it, damned good fun. Anyway, the expedition started well. In the train to Joinville Lemuffle and Pignouf had a fine time propositioning unaccompanied girls and terrorising small children, so much so that when they arrived at their destination they had worked up an enormous appetite. Clémence was very hungry too. So they found a little restaurant on the flowery banks of the Marne, installed themselves on the terrace outside and started to clamour for service.

'Anyone there?' shouted Lemuffle. 'Send for the bloody manager!'

Pignouf backed him up.

'How dare you serve us like this! I mean not serve us like this!'

Clémence, meanwhile, was quite happy stroking a big fat black cat which sat on her lap, purring in appreciation of her gentleness.

'Can I take your order, lady and gentlemen?'

An old waiter had suddenly emerged from the restaurant.

'You certainly can. What have you got to eat in this rotten dump?'

'Well, we have steaks, cutlets, etc., etc. . . .'

You don't want me to go into all these prosaic descriptive details, do you? Good.

\*         \*         \*

It may have been the poor quality of the cork, or it may have been the inefficiency of the waiter, but when he came to open the first bottle he managed to shatter the cork into a thousand fragments which all fell into the wine.

They were unforgiving.

'You . . .!' cried Lemuffle.

'You . . .!' echoed Pignouf.

(The dots represent the two most banal insults which man ever has to bear.)

The poor old waiter was most upset.

'Don't worry, don't worry,' he said. 'Look, I'll just . . . .'

He picked up a spoon and started to remove the bits of cork as he poured.

'You must be joking!' said Lemuffle wittily.

'Bring us another bottle,' said Pignouf, 'and get a bloody move on!'

But the poor old waiter appealed to their sense of decency. It seemed he wasn't on the best of terms with the manager, and if he had to report that he had wasted an entire bottle of wine through his own carelessness, he was bound to be thrown out of the restaurant. Not that he particularly liked Joinville, but he was helping to look after his little grand-daughter and he needed the money to . . . .

'What's that got to do with us? Just get another bottle! And step on it.'

Which is where Clémence intervened.

'Leave the bottle, old man,' she said in her most gentle voice. 'I'll drink it. I don't mind cork at all – in fact, I rather like it.'

The good girl was as good as her word. Despite being teased unmercifully by her two fellow boors, she drank all the wine without leaving a single crumb of cork, or without letting her smile ever leave her lips.

\*    \*    \*

And it came to pass that afternoon when the three of them went rowing on the river, their boat capsized and overturned. The two men drowned, but Clémence, made buoyant by all the cork she had consumed, floated on the surface till she was rescued by a nice young boy from a good family, recently graduated, whom she married very soon after.


# COMPANIES, INSURANCE, INFERNAL CHEEK OF

You all know my story (a minor classic by now, hence my insufferable arrogance) of the man who took his fire insurance policy literally and claimed compensation for all the firewood, candles, cigars and other combustible objects which had gone up in smoke in his house in the course of the year.

And you remember how his insurance company, not taking kindly to such actions, had him arrested and tried as a multiple arsonist?

Well, today I have another case-history for my glittering clientele which demonstrates not only that insurance companies have a steady nerve (as in the story above) but also that they have an infernal nerve (as in the story below).

At this point let me hand over to the worthy correspondent who furnished me with all the facts. (To be quite honest, I am unable to guarantee his worthiness or otherwise as I have no idea what the gentleman's name or status is, but his handwriting seems worthy enough and besides, our correspondents are always our worthy correspondents, are they not?)

Dear Sir,

May I call on the dazzling talents with which you have blinded us all for so long and ask your advice before I embark on what may well turn into a long, costly law-suit?

The facts are as follows.

I may claim without exaggeration to be one of the biggest coffee merchants in the Paris market. My job is to buy coffee in a green state, to roast it and sell it to the shops.

Well, last month in the middle of the night fire broke out in a vast suburban warehouse of mine where I had five hundred sacks of coffee in store. The building was only made of thin wood and went up like a box of matches; by the time the firemen arrived it was nothing but a smouldering ruin. Still, after the first shock had passed I thought to myself, Never mind, I'm insured, and went calmly back to bed.

A few days later the insurance experts and I met together to work out the extent of the damage. When we scoured the disaster area, we were amazed to find that the sacks of green coffee beans had not been destroyed in the fire. Not only had they not been destroyed, they had been roasted by the flames, and roasted to as fine a condition as any grocer could want.

I was busy complimenting the insurance men on the happy outcome of the incident, seeing they would now have only the warehouse to pay for, when one of them who had been jotting figures in his notebook said:

'You owe us 3,000 francs, sir.'

I thought he was joking at first. But he was quite serious.

'It costs 10 francs per sack to roast coffee. To roast 500 sacks costs 5,000 francs. Deduct 2,000 francs to cover the cost of the warehouse. That leaves 3,000 francs. You owe us 3,000 francs.'

As I stood gaping at him, he went on:

'I must remind you of the clause in your policy which says: *The insured person cannot use the insurance policy to make a profit: it can only be used to indemnify any losses sustained.* That seems clear enough to me.'

And that is how things stand at the moment. What I want to know is, should I fight their demand in court?

yours et cetera
(signature illegible)

# THE ENDS JUSTIFY THE MEANS
## A story told to Guy Cros, aged six

'Once upon a time, there was an uncle and a nephew . . . .'

'Which was which?'

'Well, the uncle was bigger than the nephew.'

'Are uncles always big, then?'

'Yes, they are, usually.'

'My uncle Henry isn't very big.'

'No, but Uncle Henry is an artist, you see.'

'Are artists always small, then?'

'Do you want to hear the story or don't you?'

'Sorry.'

'Once upon a time, there was an uncle and a nephew. The uncle was rich, *very* rich . . . .'

'How rich?'

'His income was 17,000 francs a year, but he also had lots of houses and carriages and land . . . .'

'And horses?'

'Of course. He had to have horses for the carriages.'

'What about boats? Did he have any boats?'

'Yes, he had fourteen boats.'

'Were they motor boats?'

'Three were motor boats and the rest were yachts.'

'Did he let his nephew use any of his boats?'

'Do you want to hear the story or don't you?'

'Sorry. I won't interrupt again.'

'But the nephew didn't have any money at all, which made him very sad.'

'Why didn't his uncle give him some?'

'Because the uncle was a terrible old miser who wanted to keep all his money to himself. Still, the nephew was the old man's sole heir, so . . . .'

'What does "heir" mean?'

'Well, heirs are people who come and get all your money and belongings and everything when you're dead.'

'So why didn't the nephew just kill his uncle and take it all?'

'That's a nice thing to ask, I must say! He didn't kill his uncle because you must never, *never* kill your uncle however much you want to. Even to get his belongings.'

'Why not?'

'In case the police find out.'

'But what if the police don't find out?'

'The police always find out, because the concierge always tells them. Anyway, the nephew had a better idea. He'd noticed that his uncle went very red after each meal . . . .'

'I bet he was drunk.'

'No, he just went red. He was apoplectic, you see.'

'What does aplopectic mean?'

'Apoplectic . . . it means that you have too much blood in your head and you might die if you ever got really excited about something.'

'Will that happen to me?'

'Not if I know you. Anyway, the nephew noticed that what made his uncle really bright red was listening to funny stories. Once he laughed so much he almost died.'

'Can you really die laughing?'

'Yes, if you're apoplectic . . . . So one day the nephew came to see his uncle just after dinner. The uncle had eaten even more than usual; he'd gone as red as a rooster and was puffing away like a seal . . . .'

'Like the seals we saw in the Zoo?'

'No, they were sea-lions . . . and so the nephew thought to himself: "Aha! Now's the time". And he told him a funny story, so funny that . . . .'

'Tell me the story!'

'Wait a moment, and I'll tell it you afterwards . . . anyway, the uncle listened to the story and laughed fit to burst, in fact he did burst because he died before the nephew had even finished telling it.'

'Yes, but what was the story?'

'Wait a minute . . . so, after the uncle's funeral, the nephew got everything.'

'Even the boats?'

'Yes, everything. He was the sole heir, I told you.'
'And what was the story he told his uncle?'
'It was ... it was the story I've just told you.'
'Which one?'
'You know, the one about the uncle and the nephew.'
'I don't believe it! Tell me another!'
'Not likely.'


## PS

The worst part of seeing a friend off at the station is the empty moment which comes just after the train has left. What do you do next? Well, I don't know what *you* do, and to be quite frank I don't in the least want to know, but I don't mind telling you what *I* do next. I repair immediately to the buffet of the said station and take a vermouth and cassis (not too much cassis, please) to drown my sorrow. For, as the poet hath said: 'Partir, c'est mourir un peu.'

Occasionally I find myself seeing off friends at a time of day which does not fit in with an aperitif like vermouth and cassis, and on such occasions I do not have a vermouth and cassis. I have some other drink instead. Last Tuesday, for instance, at 18.30 hours, you might have seen me sitting at a table in the buffet of the Gare de Lyon drinking an absinthe and anisette (not too much anisette, please). I had just been seeing a young lady off on the train – normally I would not dream of giving away such intimate details, but I refuse to hide anything from my readers – a young lady who was not only surpassingly beautiful but so domineering that I was only too glad to see her on her way to other climes. And I had barely had time to dip my lips in my cloudy liquor before another man sat down at the table next to me.

He promptly ordered a curaçao and bitters (not too much bitters, please) and some writing paper, and proceeded to dash off two quite different letters.

One took no time at all to write and was very soon consigned to an envelope on which he wrote the following address:–

> Colonel I A du Rabiot,
> Hôtel des Bains,
> Pourd-sur-Alaure.

But the other letter was much more trouble to write than the first one. Some phrases fell straight from his pen; others foundered after the first word. On at least two or three occasions he tore the whole letter up and started all over again. And at one point I swear I saw a tear come to his eyes and fall silently on to the station stationery beneath.

But all things must come to an end, even love letters, and when he had covered four sheets of paper in thick passionate hand-writing, the man eventually folded them up and reluctantly packed them away in a second envelope which he addressed as follows:–

> Madame Louise du R. . . .
> Poste restante
> Pourd-sur-Alaure

'Waiter!' he cried loudly. 'Bring me a couple of 3 sou stamps!'

'Sir,' said the waiter.

So far, my neighbour's features had borne all the classic signs of resigned melancholy. But without warning his face suddenly went purple with rage and he became as apoplectic as you can become without actually falling over. He wrenched the letter out of the envelope marked Mme du R. . . . and wrote on it a swift PS in the white heat of his new passion. Only two lines – but what lines they must have been! Take *that*, woman!!

By this time I felt quite intrigued by the little one-sided melo-drama, though it was pretty obvious what was afoot. The man at the next table was clearly not only a close friend of Colonel du Rabiot (who had gone off to nurse his ailments in the spa waters of P-s-A rather like Napoleon nursing his grievances on St. Helena) but also the lover of Mme du Rabiot, the beautiful wife of the Colonel. At least, I supposed she was beautiful. Between you and me, I had already fallen madly in love with the colonel's wife myself.

'Waiter!' I cried. 'Bring me a timetable, would you?'

'Sir,' said the waiter.

The next train to P-s-A was at 19.40 hours. That gave me just enough time to get a bite to eat and buy a ticket.

Pourd-sur-Alaure, in case you didn't know, is a little spa town in the hills, not very fashionable but absolutely delightful and (as the guide book inimitably says) in a marvellous setting. When I arrived at about midnight, I took a cab to the Hotel des Bains and there took a room to sleep all night dreaming of

Mme Louise du Rabiot.

The morning took a long time coming but at last the breakfast bell sounded and I went downstairs, my heart beating like a temple gong at the prospect of seeing the very same Louise du Rabiot who had inspired so many crossings out, and rewritten sentences and such a passionate PS.

I recognised her straightaway.

She was small, young, well-built, blonde and everything you could wish for. Well, not pretty perhaps, but everything else you could wish for. At any rate, she was everything *I* could wish for. She had come down to breakfast before her husband and, while waiting for him, was reading a certain letter which looked very familiar. When she came to the PS she smiled – a funny sort of smile – and tucked the letter away in her pocket. Then the Colonel lumbered in and sat down.

'I've had a letter from Alfred,' I heard her say.

'Ah?'

'He sends you lots of love.'

'Ah.'

And she shook with a long, silent, very private and discreet laugh. Then she looked up and realised that I was drinking her in with my eyes.

She did not seem in the least offended.

By lunch-time we were both on good speaking terms.

We got to know each other better in the afternoon.

By dinner time we were close friends.

After our evening together at the Casino we felt we had always known each other.

At 10 o'clock she whispered to me:

'What's the number of your hotel room?'

'17.'

'Right . . . . If you leave now, I will be with you in five minutes' time.'

In five minutes' time, she was with me.

'But your husband . . . .' I said nervously.

'Don't worry about my husband,' she said. 'He is playing whist. Do you know what the English mean when they say "whist!"?'

'Yes. It means "quiet" . . . .'

'Exactly. So keep quiet and do just what I do . . . .'

In a flash she had slipped out of her clothes.

In a second flash, she had slipped between the sheets.

In a third flash, so to speak, she was all mine.

Time for a discreet line of dots.

. . . . . . . . . . . . . . . . . . . . . . . . . . . . . . . . . . . . . . . . . . . . . . . . . . . .

When the fun and games were over, we got chatting again.

'What about Alfred, then?' I said, a bit maliciously.

'You know Alfred, do you?' she said, slightly taken aback.

'No, not at all. All I know is that he wrote a letter to you yesterday. And added a PS to it.'

'I'll say he did! It might have been quite a nice letter without that PS. Would you like to read his little PS?'

'I'd love to.'

So she showed it to me. It read:–

'PS – I've just realised what a complete fool I've been over you. I never want to see you again. As far as I'm concerned, you can go and get . . . .'

This last word was written out in full.

'Well . . .?' she said.


# THE DOCTOR
## Monologue for Cadet

For sheer nerve you can't beat a good doctor. For sheer, infernal, unbeatable nerve . . . . Nor for callousness, either.

What happens when you fall ill? You call your doctor. And he feels you all over and taps your chest and asks you a few questions – all with his mind a million miles away – then writes out a prescription and says 'I'll call in next time I'm passing'. And he passes by a few times and makes a few passes over you until it comes to pass one day that you quietly pass away.

At which point the undertaker is in like a flash to give the doctor his cut of the funeral expenses.

If you *do* manage to avoid serious illness (which isn't too hard) and stand up to his treatment (which is much more difficult), the good doctor will still be rubbing his hands with glee. Because every visit means a fee from you and a lovely commission from your chemist and it all snowballs very soon into a small fortune for him.

The only thing that makes a doctor sad is when you recover immediately. Even then he puts a brave face on it and has the infernal cheek to say:

'Good! good! Caught you just in time.'

I have known some doctors with the most infernal nerve, but the worst of the lot is my own doctor. My ex-doctor, rather, because I have just given him the push. And believe me, *I'm* not the loser.

It all began one day when I woke up in a cold sweat, or maybe a hot sweat, I can never tell the difference, and realised I had caught something nasty. So, as I have a healthy regard for myself – what do you expect? I'm the only one I've got – I phoned my doctor immediately and he arrived within the hour.

I wasn't feeling very well when he arrived. By the time he had gone I felt awful. I took to my bed at once.

More visits. More medicine. More symptoms than ever.

Within a few days I was kilos lighter and pounds poorer.

Then one morning when I was feeling absolutely wretched my doctor examined me rather more thoroughly than usual and said:

'Quite happy in this flat, are you?'

'Yes, I suppose so.'

'How much rent do you pay?'

'Three thousand four hundred a year.'

'The concierge seems all right, does he?'

'No complaints so far.'

'How about the landlord?'

'The landlord is very reasonable, actually.'

'Good. Do you get any trouble from smoking chimneys?'

'Not really.'

And so on and so forth.

Till I began to wonder: What is the brute driving at? I can understand him being interested in the humidity or otherwise of my quarters, seeing how ill I am, but why on earth should he take any interest in the amount of rent I have to pay? So, weak as I was, I felt impelled to ask:

'What are all these questions in aid of, doctor?'

'To be quite frank,' he said, 'I'm looking for a new flat and yours is just the sort of place I'm after.'

'Yes, but I have no intention of moving out of here . . . .'

'Perhaps not, but you may have to in the very near future.'

'Move? But why?

'Ah! Well . . . .'

Suddenly I twigged.

My doctor thought I was for it, and was trying to tell me so in no uncertain terms.

I can hardly tell you what effect this curt revelation had on me.
A terrible sort of stage fright, to begin with.

Followed very shortly by a blind rage. What a way to treat a
sick man, I thought! Not just any old sick man, either, but a
customer! A *good* customer at that.

So you'd like my flat would you, my friend? Nothing doing!

*         *         *

If *you* ever fall ill, I can recommend my own course of treatment
to you. Work yourself up into a tremendous rage. It may not do
you much good, but it certainly cured *me*.

I kicked my doctor down the stairs.

I threw his prescriptions out of the window.

(When I say I threw them out of the window, I'm exaggerating
slightly. I don't like scattering broken glass around because that
could hurt passers-by and I don't like hurting the man in the
street – what do you take me for? A *doctor*?)

What I acutally did was send back the offending medicaments
to the chemist accompanied by a stiff letter.

My God, I have never seen so many bottles and packets and
jars in all my life!

I had been given so many prescriptions that on one occasion I
had got the doctor's orders all wrong; I had slapped a linctus on
my stomach and swallowed a dressing.

It was the only time I had ever felt at all better.

And when the whole episode was over I renewed the lease on
my flat. And let my option on a new doctor lapse.


# LIONISATION

In our last issue I courageously published an article in which I
mercilessly flayed the vile activities of our funeral undertakers. I
revealed their attempts to corrupt the concierges of France and
proved irrefutably that they are inciting the latter to murder their
tenants in return for a hefty commission on the burial expenses.

It brought me a heavy mailbag.

Mainly foul insults and gross libels from the tradesmen in question.

And a good many indignant protests from our friends the concierges who swore blind that never, never would they conceive the

slightest designs on the life of the humblest tenant (oh how little I knew about concierges!) even if it meant them earning enough to last them the rest of their days.

But also a few very interesting ideas on the subject from my readers, to whom I am alas unable to offer the royal welcome they deserve on account of the miserly space allotted to us writers.

I am therefore restricted to publishing only one of these epistles.

*To the Editor-in-Chief*
Sir,
On behalf of right-minded people of all parties, I welcome the masterly way in which you have exposed the dangerous dealings of these macabre tradesmen who make their living from other people's deaths.

But is there any solution to this disgraceful scandal?

Yes, sir, there is. There is one solution and one only, to wit:

The banning of all funerals.

I know that when I urge an immediate stop to *all* kinds of funeral service I am asking for the impossible, but at least let us take immediate steps to change funeral undertaking from a scandalous private industry into a dignified public service.

If I were something in the government, I would make a start by doing everything in my power to do away with the barbarous custom whereby we so brutally let our deceased putrefy in the foul humus of our cemeteries.

I find the system of cremation equally unappealing.

You yourself, my dear M. Allais, have in the past suggested an ingenious alternative. As far as I can recall, it involved treating the corpse with a solution of nitric and sulphuric acids, much in the same way as guncotton is made, then transforming the dear departed into a spectacular firework show.

Very exciting, I admit, but – between you and me – not very dignified.

My own approach is quite different. I visualise nothing more or less than the disposal of our corpses by means of hungry lions.

I think you will agree that the ceremony thus involved would be most picturesque and would even have a certain grandeur.

The only drawback to my proposed method – and I am the first to admit it – is that lions have an unconquerable aversion to meat which has gone off in the slightest, which means that it would be preferable to deliver the body for the ceremony a few hours before it had breathed its last. (A few days before, if possible.)

I would be pleased to hear what you, as editor-in-chief, think of
my little suggestion.

I remain etc. (there then follows the signature of a famous name
which, for the sake of his family, I prefer not to reveal).

What do I think of your little suggestion. M. Poincaré?

I will tell you.

You are a puller of legs, sir, and if I had bothered to read your
letter to the end before attaching it to my copy, as I so foolishly
failed to do, I would never have done you the honour of printing
your contribution, believe you me.

It's too late now, alas.

# THE CORPSE CAR

You may recently have read a piece of fantasy by Tristan Bernard
in these very pages in which he posited the invention of an electrical device for removing the droppings left by rocking-horses.

No doubt you smiled to yourself and passed on. Well, the problem doesn't affect you personally, I'm sure.

But I can think of a good many people, solid worthy citizens all,
who will have found his little joke cruelly near the truth.

I refer to the genuine sweepers of real droppings left by live
horses.

Not so long ago I had a long talk with the genial head of the
*National Federation of Horse Dropping Sweepers* (*Seine Branch*) and I
learnt from him that the livelihood of these good men is becoming
highly precarious.

Why?

You all know why.

Because of bicycles and cars!

They are the culprits.

For – and it would be childish to deny it any longer – the horse
is not only dying, it is already dead. Henceforth the noblest friend
of man is destined to be the petrol-driven vehicle made by Mes-
sieurs Dion and Bouton.

True, the Society for the Protection of Animals could recently
be heard praising the advent of the car on the grounds that it
would relieve their poor nags of such unwanted drudgery. But

these otherwise kindly gents of the SPA are too short-sighted to realise that what may be good for animals is bad for long-suffering humanity.

What will the horse droppings sweepers do instead?

What will the spur-makers do?

What will the merchants of riding boots do?

And what will happen to all those industries which may seem far removed from the training and equipping of horses but which will be just as savagely affected by the scourge of this modern invention?

Have you thought, to name only one example, of the effect on undertakers and their horse-drawn hearses? They are, after all, the *only* tradesmen who we all have to patronise sooner or later. What, I ask you, will be the effect on *them*!

Luckily, it so happens by sheer chance that I am at present involved in the promotion of a new invention which will solve the problems of all undertakers, because it will replace the horse-drawn funeral hearse *and* the cremation oven at one and the same time.

The necromobile!

(Following the fashion of the day, the inventor of the machine has given it an English name: 'Corpse Car'.)

As you may have perhaps guessed already, the energy necessary to drive the vehicle is derived from the burning of the body of the dear departed. This means that the engine is powered both by steam and gas via a somewhat complicated process. The steam comes from the water content of the late dear one (the human body is, unbelievably, 75% water). The gas is derived from the distillation of the rest of the remains of the poor lamented father (or mother, as the case may be).

My inventor calculates that a dead man of average weight should provide enough fuel to carry at least a dozen funeral guests to a cemetery eight kilometres away.

Which means that at last it will be possible to be simultaneously quick and dead.

# CAPTAIN CAP AGAIN

Arriving in Nice for the first time, two large posters on a wall caught the eye of Captain Cap and myself.

(I can't help thinking there is something terribly wrong with the syntax of that sentence. It is hard to believe I was once a promising writer.)

The poster that I liked read as follows:

> MONSIEUR X ———— CHIROPODIST
> Address . . . . . . . . . . . Telephone Number . . . .
> 'The only reputable chiropodist in Nice'

Never in my life have I so regretted not having a single corn, verruca, bunion or trace of athlete's foot in my netherest regions.

Can you imagine? There I was, within reach of a master crafts-man who not only prided himself on his reputation but could con-fidently state that he was the only chiropodist in the metropolis of Nice who could legitimately claim onc – and I had nothing to offer him on which to work his skill. Pity (what a, oh!).

The only constructive suggestion Captain Cap could make was that he seemed to remember that among the womenfolk of some Polynesian archipelago or other it was the custom to measure one's beauty by the amount of corns found in the most unexpected parts of the body and that if I liked we could adjourn to the chiropodist to have me examined. I politely declined.

Cap himself was much more interested in the other advertise-ment, which announced to All and Sundry (no doubt a firm of passers-by) that anyone having a sum between 25 centimes and 1 franc on their person could gain admittance to a private view of an orang-outang, yes, ladies and gentlemen, the genuine wild man of the woods, the ONLY (just like my chiropodist, only more so) the ONLY orang-outan ever seen in France since time immemorial! The inscription continued: 'His name is Auguste. We shall gladly give 10,000 francs to anyone who can disprove our claim.'

10,000 francs! But for disproving what? That he was a genuine orang-outan? Or that he really was called Auguste?

To Captain Cap's pure and unsuspecting soul, there could be no doubt. All one had to do was prove that the pathetic creature was *not* called Auguste, collect the 10,000 francs and rush off to break the bank at Monte Carlo. How lovely and simple it all seemed to him.

And thereafter Cap kept muttering unendingly to me:

'I don't know why, but something keeps telling me that that orang-outan does not rejoice under the name of Auguste.'

'Oh, forget it.'

'Why should I forget it? You saw his picture. He doesn't even *look* like an Auguste.'

'**** off.'

'Allais, your taste is objectionable. If you tell me once more to **** off, I shall find myself giving you a ******* good kick in the *****.'

My motto in life is that there are few things worse you can get in the ***** than a ******* good kick. So I changed the subject and bought Cap a Manhattan Cocktail.

That same evening, Cap returned to Antibes to spend the night on his yacht and it was another fortnight before I saw him again.

One morning he burst into my bedroom before I had even woken up, shouting at me in a most unhealthy sort of way:

'I've got it! I've got it at last! I have absolute, definite proof!'

'Proof?' I said in my sleep. 'Proof of what?'

'I knew all along that bloody orang-outang wasn't called Auguste!'

'Ah!'

'I have here in my hand a telegram from Borneo, from the place where he was born. And guess what? Not only is he not called Auguste – his real name is William!'

'Would that make him a relation of William of Orang?'

'Allais, your taste is still objectionable. No matter – we now have from the French consul in Borneo all the evidence we need to prove beyond doubt that he is not Auguste. Let us to a lawyer and claim our 10,000 francs.'

My solicitor in Nice, M. Pineau, one of the most eminent lawmen this side of the Alps, arranged the paperwork in the twinkling of an eye and off we set to claim our reward.

Alas! We found the travelling fair had packed its bags and travelled on. There was no sign of the soi-disant Auguste, or his tent, or the owner, or even the 10,000 francs. They had all moved to San Remo in Italy. And I need hardly remind my readers that under Italian law any monkey, chimpanzee or ape more than 70 centimetres tall may legally be known by any name he chooses.

# A STROKE OF GOOD LUCK

A few days ago I was involved in a most delightful adventure which I insist on sharing with my distinguished circle of readers. On the day in question, as a matter of fact, I had spent most of my spare time sitting in the Law Courts, but I became so power-fully affected by the eloquent pleading of the counsel for my de-fence that I could no longer resist the urge to dash across to the Brasserie Dreher for a large glass of beer. And it was there, after only a couple of minutes, that I realised I was being closely observed by a tall young man, with a pale sad face. So I wasn't too surprised when he got up, came over and very politely:

'Could I steal a few moments of your valuable time?'

'Of course,' I said. 'Sit down.'

'I have been watching you, and I get the impression that you are a man who would not be surprised by anything human be-haviour had to offer.'

'That just about sums me up.'

'I thought as much. In that case, you may be sympathetic to what I am about to ask of you. You see ... well, I won't bother with any preamble, or foreword or introduction. All I need tell you is that I have fallen madly in love with a girl who comes past this place every evening at about half past six. So far I have never dared speak to her, because I am desperately shy. But this morning I took a solemn oath that I would go out and talk to her *today!* The question is, how? Well, I have decided to use one of the oldest tricks in the world. Which means, of course, one of the best tried tricks in the world.'

'Tell me more.'

'What I suggest is that when she appears over the skyline, I point her out to you, and you, as soon as she comes close enough, go out and accost her. You know, make one or two rather forward suggestions ... then become a bit more pressing ... then go the whole hog. As soon as *I* see her getting flustered and embarrassed, I shall come to the rescue. "Sir", I shall wax indignant, "I must ask you to leave this young lady alone!" etc., etc. After that it should be plain sailing.'

'Excellent!'

'At which point you retire from the scene crestfallen and discomfited. I shall be glad to let you know what ensues thereafter, if you accept my invitation to dine with me here at midday tomorrow.'

'I gladly agree.'

'Good. Ah! . . . here she comes now.'

The young lady in question was certainly very presentable, very presentable indeed. So, following the plan of action, I went out and fell in step beside her. 'Hello, darling, any chance of . . .?' and so on and so forth. She didn't say a word. My questions became a little franker, but that pretty mouth remained tight shut. So my conversation became, well, somewhat ungentlemanly. She looked prettier and more desirable as each moment passed. At last the pale sad young man thought it was time to interfere.

'Sir, I must ask you to leave this young lady alone!'

At which she turned on him with a furious expression and, in the most urban of accents:

'Well, you've got a bleedin' nerve, ain't you? Who asked you to poke your nose in?'

And to me:

'Go on, tell 'im to clear off! Give 'im one if 'e doesn't!'

I debated whether the script really called for physical violence.

'Well? Go on, knock 'is block off! Blimey, are you a man or ain't yer?'

This lingering doubt about my virility made up my mind for me. I took a long powerful swing at the pale sad young man, which he managed to parry neatly with his left eye . . . . Not an hour later this delicious child, this veritable Vermicelli* virgin, was ushering me into her apartment on the Boulevard Arago prior to one of the most intimate and enjoyable evenings of my life.

\*     \*     \*

The next day, on the stroke of twelve, I appeared for my lunchtime rendezvous with the pale sad young man.

He never turned up.

Ingratitude, perhaps? Or just plain forgetfulness?

---

\*Famous nineteenth century Italian painter.

# A CHRISTMAS STORY II

I think I am speaking for fellow burglars everywhere when I say that my favourite day in the year – or, to be strictly accurate, my favourite night of the year – is Christmas Eve.

Especially if I am out burgling in the country.

In certain parts of the country, especially.

By which I mean (I don't have to spell all this out for you, do I?) those parts of the country where religion is still a devout and flourishing business.

Because there are in France to this day, believe it or not, naive rural areas where the inhabitants flock to midnight mass on Christmas Eve not merely from a sense of duty but with a genuine fervour. They go, not so much as Christians to prayer, more as poets to embrace the images of their dreams. The star ... the three wise men ... the stable ... baby Jesus on his bed of soft wood shavings ... pretty little Mary, Mummy of God, flushed with excitement yet a bit pale too; well, after all, it's so tiring having to entertain all these unexpected guests, look after them, chat to them, see them out ... and old carpenter Joseph in the corner, looking rather overcome, feeling ever so slightly out of place (not that he hasn't been amply compensated since with a nice permanent niche in the Abode of the Blessed) ....

*     *     *

Time: the eighteen-hundred-and-ninety-third anniversary of the great event.

Place: the parish of A-on-B (in the Département of C-on-D).

It was a foul night.

The sky was full of stars.

Not a cloud to be seen anywhere.

There was even a big, round, full moon. Stupid great thing! I felt as if I was in a hall of mirrors with all the lights on and the chandeliers blazing overtime.

How would *you* like to work in such terrible conditions?

Still, I had one thing in my favour. The place I was about to patronise was fully equipped with plenty of jewels, silver, stocks and shares, all in the same drawer, together with a little book containing their numbers carefully noted down. (When will they ever learn?)

I would have to go in by the back garden. Unfortunately, there was a large dog there. Fortunately, strychnine has many valuable uses . . . what am I saying? Strychnine has *one* valuable use.

While I was waiting for mass to start, I went over my plan of operations again. A lovely plan it was, worked out for me by a friend who till recently was an officer in the Corps of Engineers but had to leave suddenly for reasons which are none of your business.

A little beauty of a plan.

A blind burglar could have got away with it.

And to think there are some people who disapprove of sending army officers to college.

At last, midnight came.

The bell rang for mass.

Then, silence.

Everyone was safely in church.

*       *       *

'Yap, yap, yap yap!'

Shut up, you mangy cur.

'Are you hungry, then? Here's a nice little pill for a nice little doggy.'

He keeled over and lay on his back, four little paws sticking up in the air, observing a religious silence.

And there I was, inside!

*       *       *

There I was, inside.

And even more quickly, there I was making for the roof.

Because from nowhere a man had appeared with a pistol in his hand, looking much more intent on arresting people than on celebrating the birth of his Saviour.

He shouted at me like a madman.

I ran like a madman.

'After him, after him!' he screamed.

And after me came a great mob of coppers, firemen and God knows what else.

I never enjoy scrambling around on rooftops at the best of times, but when it has been snowing hard the whole thing becomes un-utterably melancholy, don't you find? I do.

Suddenly there was a great cry of triumph from everybody: 'Got you! Got you! Come on, you old rascal, come quietly!'

Which was odd. Because it wasn't me they'd got.

So who was it, then?

I risked a little peep from the chimneystack behind which I was squatting.

The police were holding on to the arms, legs and head of some poor old chap who was struggling away for dear life.

And I felt very sorry for him.

Because the man they had mistaken for me, the man they thought was the burglar, the man in the long white beard and red cloak bringing presents from baby Jesus, was none other than Father Christmas.

# THE SEARCH FOR THE UNKNOWN WOMAN

When I give a young person the benefit of my advice, there is one thing I always stress above all. If you intend to embark on an act of violence or a serious crime, *plan it carefully*. Otherwise the results may be more complicated than you anticipate. Let me tell you a little story to show you what I mean.

Once upon a time, there was a nice young man (a bit impressionable, perhaps, but nice and young) who was attending the funeral of a lady who had just died and had been, up to that very moment, the wife of a friend of his. Our young man was not particularly religious-minded, so his attitude towards the service could best be described as inattentive, with perhaps a jigger of boredom. When, suddenly . . .

No sarcastic laughs, please. Which one of us can be sure that such a thing will not happen to him?

When suddenly . . .

You might say that the human heart is a bit like the solar system. They are both subject to bombardment from meteors, shooting stars, flashes of light . . .

Because suddenly the hero of our story felt something land in his emotio-cardiac network. To wit, a thunderbolt.

He had just noticed, across the aisle on the ladies' side, not two yards away, the most ravishing creature that God had ever seen fit to deposit on this planet. Shall I describe her full glory to you?

No, I shall not. It would be a waste of time and energy. Not that I could tell you if she was fair or plain, had dark, brown or light eyes, or if her hair was blue, green or violet, because I never set eyes on her. Nor does it matter. The only important thing is that our poor hero had been struck by a thunderbolt, the famous thunderbolt called true love.

'That woman,' he barely had the strength to say to himself, 'that woman is, from now on, the only person who can make my life worth living.'

And he swore to find out immediately who she was and to marry her. Well, if not to marry her, at least to make her his. And if she were married already, then to steal her from her husband.

But after the service, while our young man was still shaking his friend's hand in the vestry, the unknown woman disappeared. Disappeared! Desperately he rushed to the entrance of the church, ran through the whole place, looked everywhere, refusing to believe that she had gone. He stayed there till night came, hoping wildly against hope that she would suddenly emerge from the shadows and throw herself into his arms crying: 'I love you too! Let us run away together to the Aegean!'

It was no use. Darkness fell and there was still no sign of her.

The next day it became light again, then later darkness fell again, and so on alternately. He kept looking for her everywhere and found her nowhere.

Eventually, in his despair, he decided to work out the problem very coldly and logically.

'Whoever she was, she came to my friend's wife's funeral. So she is obviously a friend of his family. That means that if my friend died, she would come to his funeral as well. Therefore, if I kill my friend, I shall see her again.'

He killed his friend. But he did not see her again. Because, sad to say, a few days after the murder some gentleman from the police force came to detain him and a few months after that some other gentlemen of the law found him guilty and condemned him to death after a trial conducted with the utmost impartiality. Not that he cared, as he was only too happy to be rid of an existence which had by then lost any meaning for him.

So he was already striding happily towards the guillotine on the last morning when suddenly he stopped and gave a great cry.

As you may know, members of the public are very occasionally admitted to beheadings if they receive special authorisation, and on this occasion there was, as well as all those normally in attendance, a young lady present.

It was none other than his unknown woman!

And about bloody time, too.

# ABSINTHE

Five o'clock.

Rotten weather. Grey sky ... dreary, mind-chilling sort of grey.

Oh for a short, sharp shower to get rid of all these stupid people milling around like walking clichés .... Rotten weather.

Another bad day today, dammit. Devilish luck.

Article rejected. So politely, though:

'Liked your article ... interesting idea ... nicely written ... but not really in the style of the magazine, I'm afraid ....'

Style of the magazine? Magazine's *style*?? Dullest magazine in the whole of Paris! Whole of France.

Publisher preoccupied, distrait, mind elsewhere.

'Got your manuscript here somewhere ... yes, liked your novel ... interesting idea ... nicely written ... but business is very slow at the moment, you see ... already got too much stuff on our hands ... ever thought of writing something aimed more at the market? Lots of sales ... fame ... honours list ....'

Went out nodding politely, feeling stupid:

'Some other time perhaps.'

Rotten weather. Half past five.

The boulevards! Let's take to the boulevards. Might meet a friend or two. If you can call them friends. Load of worthless .... But who *can* you trust in Paris?

And why is everyone out tonight so *ugly*?

The women so badly dressed. The men looking so stupid.

'Waiter! Bring me an absinthe and sugar!'

Good fun, watching the sugar lump melt very quietly on its little filter as the absinthe gradually trickles over it. Same way they say a drip of water hollows out granite. Only difference, sugar softer than granite. Just as well, too. Can you imagine? Waiter, one absinthe and granite!

Absinthe on the rocks! That's a good one, that's a good one. Very funny. For people who aren't in a hurry – absinthe and granite! Nice one.

Sugar lump's almost melted now. There it goes. Just like us. Striking image of mankind, a sugar lump . . . .

When we are dead, we shall all go the same way. Atom by atom, molecule by molecule. Dissolved, dispersed, returned to the Great Beyond by kind permission of earthworms and the vegetable kingdom.

Everything for the best then. Victor Hugo and the meanest hack equal in the eyes of the Great God Maggot. Thank goodness.

Rotten weather . . . . Bad day. Fool of an editor. Unbelievable ass of a publisher.

Don't know, though. Perhaps not so much talent as keep telling self.

Nice stuff, absinthe. Not the first mouthful, perhaps. But after that.

Nice stuff.

Six o'clock. Boulevards looking a bit more lively now. And look at the women!

A lot prettier than an hour ago. Better dressed, too. Men don't look so cretinous either.

Sky still grey. Nice mother-of-pearl sort of grey. Rather effective. Lovely nuances. Setting sun tingeing the clouds with pale coppery pink glow. Very fine.

'Waiter! An absinthe and anis!'

Good fun, absinthe with sugar, but can't hang around all day waiting for it to melt.

Half past six.

All these women! And so pretty, most of them. And so strange too.

Mysterious, rather.

Where do they all come from? Where are they all going to? Ah, shall we ever know!

Not one of them spares me a glance – and yet I love them all so much.

I look at each one as she passes, and her features are so burnt on my mind that I know I will never forget her to my dying day. Then she vanishes, and I have absolutely no recollection what she looked like.

Luckily, there are always prettier girls following behind.

And I would love them so, if only they would let me! But they all pass by. Shall I ever see any of them again?

Street-hawkers out there on the pavement, selling everything under the sun. Newspapers . . . celluloid cigar-cases . . . cuddly toy monkeys – any colour you want . . . .

Who *are* all these men? The flotsam of life, no doubt. Unrecognised geniuses. Renegades. Eyes full of strange depths.

A book waiting to be written about them. A great book. An unforgettable book. A book that everyone would have to buy – everyone!

Oh, these women!

Why doesn't it occur to just one of them to come in and sit down beside me . . . kiss me very gently . . . caress me . . . take me in her arms and rock me to and fro just as mother did when I was small?

'Waiter! An absinthe, neat. And make it a big one!'

# THE CORK

Many funny things happened to my friend Léon Dumachin on his honeymoon but none funnier than the adventure that befell him in Kleinberg.

\*      \*      \*

We spent two or three days in Munich (Dumachin speaking) and then announced our intention of moving on to Kleinberg, which is a lovely little spot. But when a friend of ours at Munich heard our plans he looked hard at me and then looked at my wife and then burst into a great fit of silent laughter, with his Bavarian sauerkraut stomach shaking up and down.

'What's so funny about the idea of going to Kleinberg?' I inquired.

'Well, if you *are* going to Kleinberg,' said the furniture-stealer (a patriotic reference to 1870), 'you will almost certainly be staying at the Three Kings Hotel.'

'That is indeed the place we have chosen.'

'And they will almost certainly put you in the big first floor bedroom.'

'I couldn't say.'

'I could, though. They always give that room to young marrieds on their honeymoon.'

'Ah.'

'Quite so. Well, watch out for the cork . . . .'

'Cork? What cork?'

'You don't know about the famous cork trick, then?'

'I don't think I've ever . . . .'

So the good citizen of Munich told me all about the cork trick.

It seems that the room they keep ready at the Three Kings for honeymoon couples is positioned exactly above a little ground floor room and that this little ground floor room is a bar which is frequented every night by a select group of Kleinberg tradesmen.

To the head of the bed is attached a length of string which passes through a hole bored in the floor and then dangles from the ceiling of the bar below.

At the end of the string there is a cork.

Do you get the picture?

The slightest movement of the bed sets the string in motion, which in turn starts the cork off on a wild dance.

You can imagine the stolid citizens of Kleinberg sitting there all evening, smoking, drinking and impassively watching the lunatic antics of the cork.

A little jump to begin with, as the lady gets into bed.

A bigger movement to denote the arrival of the gentleman.

And then . . . et cetera, et cetera.

Apparently the sight of the silently gambolling cork is so riveting that the beer-drinkers of the Three Kings sometimes stay till sunrise.

I was profusely grateful to our conqueror (another 1870 reference) for his revelations and promised not to draw the attention of the men of Kleinberg to myself and my wife.

At the same time, I couldn't help feeling that I had no right to deprive these good people of their innocent amusement.

So I compromised with an ingenious solution which I still to this day feel proud of.

\*          \*          \*

Everything turned out just as predicted.

When we arrived that evening at the Three Kings I saw at first glance that we had indeed been given the room above the little ground floor bar.

I established at second glance that the sensitive piece of string was in position, waiting.

And I could see downstairs, in my mind's eye, that piece of cork, motionless for the time being, yet destined soon to leap into the wildest cavorting. I could also see the expectant upturned faces of the men of Kleinberg, doubly expectant on this occasion, no doubt, at the thought that their entertainment was to be provided by a French team.

So to the great bafflement of Amélie (who knew nothing of all this) I lay flat on the floor equipped with a pair of scissors and our travelling clock.

Taking the greatest care not to twitch the string and arouse suspicions downstairs, I cut it free from the bed and attached the end to the tip of the minute hand of the clock, which I placed next to the hole.

There!

Can you picture the scene?

All those good people downstairs, smoking their pipes and supping from their tankards, sitting all evening watching the cork go slowly, slowly up and slowly, slowly down again.

I have no idea what went through their German minds.

But I am told that by six o'clock in the morning half Kleinberg was in the bar with their eyes fixed on the all-revealing cork.

I'm afraid they must have thought that the reputation of the French as great lovers was somewhat exaggerated.


# LITTORALLY

Every summer I like to betake myself to a secluded watering-place where I can let my shattered body recover from the thousand and one excesses of the previous winter, and this year I have come to Gadouville-sur-Mer. Not many people have heard of it, but it boasts one of the most delightful beaches to be found anywhere in the world. It has everything – sand like spun gold, luxurious vegetation, picturesque surroundings, friendly natives, even well brought up bailiffs. A second garden of Eden, in fact.

To add to its natural attractions the town can also boast one millionaire, one war hero and one eccentric, and as I have nothing better to do this morning I shall write a little piece (I am after all paid to write little pieces)* to tell you how the millionaire of Gadouville-sur-Mer got his million, the war hero got his medal and the eccentric got his reputation.

*          *          *

* (Paid very little, I may say.)

The millionaire is, or was, a young man from Le Havre who once upon a time worked as an apprentice for a ship-builder there, since dead (in prison). While the young man was still earning no more than 120 francs a month, an old aunt of his in Fécamp died and left him several thousand francs. Pausing only to give the lady a decent burial, the young man left ship-building for good and plunged recklessly into commodity speculation. Madly he bought quantities of coffee 'at a fair price', cotton 'middling cheap' etc., etc., etc., and then sold them again. And as he took great care always to sell them at a somewhat higher price than he had bought them, there was always a little surplus left over for our hero, or what the English call an 'element of profit'.

As the process took place every day over a long period, the several thousand francs which came from the old lady of Fécamp soon turned into a great deal more and nobody was more pleased by this, in her absence, than her young nephew.

But one day our speculating hero got an unpleasant surprise when a cashier at his bank, by the name of Loripeau, decamped for other shores, taking with him among other things ten thousand francs belonging to our friend. No doubt thinking that the neighbourhood of Le Havre would be too hot for him for a time, Loripeau had decided to indulge in a change of climate. How sad that in the haste of his departure he took with him a cash box belonging to his employers which he no doubt mistook for his hat box! And that by another frightful mischance, the cash box happened to be particularly full that day.

When the young speculator heard the news, he leapt into action. He changed, shot down to the harbour and made inquiries of anyone who might know where Loripeau had gone – dockers, customs officials, all and sundry (Co. Ltd.). And soon he found out what he wanted to know. A customs man had seen Loripeau boarding the *Ville d'Elboeuf*, a merchant ship bound for Buenos Aires.

Five minutes later, the following conversation took place between our friend and the captain of the *Belle Anais*.

'Are you the Captain?'

'Yes; can I help you?'

'Will you be sailing for Buenos Aires soon?'

'Next week.'

'Could I persuade you to leave tonight?'

'Not a chance. I haven't started loading yet.'

'Never mind, I'd compensate you for any lost cargo. All I want to know is whether your boat can go as fast as the *Ville d'Elboeuf*.'

'We're about evenly matched. But . . .'

'And with extra sail?'

'With extra sail I could overhaul her. But . . .'

'If you get to Buenos Aires before she does, I'll give you 10,000 francs.'

Using all her spare canvas the *Belle Anais* got to Buenos Aires forty-eight hours before the *Ville d'Elboeuf*. When the *Ville d'Elboeuf* docked, our young friend from Le Havre was hiding behind a huge pile of raw hide on the quay and from this vantage point had the great satisfaction of seing Loripeau disembark with a large suitcase in his hand. No sooner had Loripeau registered at a hotel and got to his room than he was surprised to hear a knock at the door.

'Come in!' he cried, with no idea who might be calling on him in South America.

Unlike you and me.

'Morning, Loripeau. Have a nice crossing?'

Loripeau could not have looked more thunderstruck if he had been struck by thunder; lightning, rather.

Our young friend from Le Havre drew a pistol or two casually from his pocket and said:

'I'd like my 10,000 francs back, please.'

'Here you are,' said Loripeau, very pale.

'And the 10,000 francs I had to pay the captain of the *Belle Anais* to persuade him to catch you up.'

'There you are.'

'Thank you. Oh, and another 10,000 francs to cover the expense of compensating the captain of the said *Belle Anais* for his lost cargo.'

'There you are.'

'Thank you. And another 10,000 francs to cover the personal inconvenience you have caused me.'

'There.'

'That makes 40,000 in all, for which I am very grateful to you.'

'That . . . that's all?'

'Just one other thing . . . . A small business proposition.'

'Yes?'

'I've been looking round Buenos Aires and there's a fortune to be made in the leather trade. How would you like to go into partnership with me here?'

'Suits me.'

There certainly was a fortune to be made in leather, because ten years later the young man from Le Havre (no longer so young by then) returned across the sea to France with at least a million francs in his pocket and settled in Gadouville-sur-Mer, where he built up the estate he now lives on and which is the admiration of every tourist. Now he is one of the great local figures; only last year he married off his daughter to the local *député*, a politician somewhat to the right of centre who can safely be said to be a credit to public life.

*       *       *

And there I must take leave of you, I am afraid; my dinner gong has just sounded.

The story of Gadouville-sur-Mer's war hero and its eccentric will have to wait till another time.

Bon appétit.


# THE BEAUTIFUL STRANGER

He was just wandering down the boulevard Malesherbes when it happened, wandering along with his hands in his pockets and his thoughts far away, so far away in fact that he could not properly be said to be thinking at all.

And then, as I say, it happened. He passed a woman he recognised going the other way.

(If I go into a description of her, it will only hold up the story. Just conjure up a mental image of the kind of woman who appeals to you, and that will be quite good enough.)

As she passed, he automatically tipped his hat to her, but got no response whatsoever. Funny, he thought. Was it because she hadn't recognised him? Or simply because she hadn't noticed his small friendly gesture? Either way, he had definitely got no response at all.

Which was strange, because he was sure he had met her somewhere before. But where the hell had it been? And when? Well, whoever she was, she was certainly a damned attractive girl.

He walked on for about twenty yards, then suddenly realised he couldn't leave it at that. He simply had to turn round, catch her up and take another look. So he did.

She looked familiar from behind as well.

Where the hell *had* he seen her before? And when had it been?

He followed her along the boulevard till they came to the Avenue de Villiers which she took as far as the Square de Trafalgar. Then she turned right.

Carefully keeping his distance behind her, the man suddenly thought to himself: How very strange – this is getting quite near where I live. But he still couldn't place where he had met her, or when.

The mysterious woman walked along the rue Albert Tartempion until she reached No. 21 and went in. This was too much! She was actually going into the building where he lived!

She got into the empty lift and went up.

He raced up the stairs after her, four at a time.

The lift stopped at the fourth floor. His floor.

She walked along the corridor and stopped at his door. Was she going to ring the bell? No, she wasn't. Because she calmly took out a key and opened the door.

A burglar!

He leapt forward to challenge her.

'Hello,' she said. 'You're home early.'

Then he remembered where he had seen her before, and when it had been.

She was his wife.

# M.E.R.
## or
# THE NEW AMERICAN
# MOTO-ELEVATED-ROAD

As I can't be everywhere at the same time, I was unable to attend any of the main events in the recent French motor-racing season, because I had been kindly invited by a group of American car-makers to go over to their country and be a guest at one of the most interesting races I have ever attended: the 'Rocky Mountain Cup'. It does not seem to have been reported anywhere in the French press, though I am not sure why. Was it perhaps because the results were not quite so sensational as the organisers had hoped? Forty-three machines entered for the race, and no less than forty-three crossed the startling-line, which is good going; the only disappointing thing was the none of them crossed the finishing-line.

Fourteen of them managed to collide with the picturesque rocks after which the race is named.

Eleven safely avoided the rocks and plunged into an assortment of ravines, gorges and waterfalls.

And the remaining eighteen chose quite the wrong moment to encounter a herd of buffalo moving at high speed in the opposite direction. Not that a head-on meeting between car and animal will necessarily be a disaster for the driver, because a motor car in good condition on a well maintained highway will always beat, say, a large spaniel and indeed convert it instantly into a respectable hearth rug. A herd of bison is a different proposition, though, especially as statisticians tell us that bison never move round in groups of less than 170,000. Eighteen motor cars are no match for 170,000 or more bison, as we found when we visited the scene of the accident the day after it happened. There was, of course, no sign of the buffalo herd by then. Nor of the eighteen motor cars. Anyone who has been privileged to witness the purée into which 170,000 bison (or 680,000 bisons' hooves) can turn eighteen motor cars has a pretty good idea of the concept of nothingness. Perhaps I understand why the organisers of the race were less than eager to seek world-wide publicity for the American car industry.

But if you think that they were discouraged, you don't know the Americans. They were twice as determined after that to find some way of guaranteeing fast, safe motoring. No halfway measures for them, either; they decided that as the earth's surface was obviously unsafe for driving, they would look elsewhere. The flat open road may be all right for horses, cripples, Europeans and snails, they said, but we Yankees can drive in the air!

So they immediately decided to build the Moto-Elevated-Road. What is the M.E.R., as it is already familiarly known?

The name gives away the basic secret, of course, but it gives no idea of the fiendish ingenuity which will enable the Americans to criss-cross their country with thousands of light aerial motorways which will, very soon, be teeming with small American cars.

Now, the first thing that the average Frenchman notices when he arrives in the U.S.A. is the almost incredible quantity of telegraph wires overhead. In this country we are used to seeing only one or two together, or a dozen at most, but over in Uncle Sam's own country it isn't unusual to see a hundred or more at a time.

When I say telegraph wires, of course, I mean other kinds of wires as well, such as electricity supply wires, telephone wires, overhead cables and so on.

They are all arranged one above the other, in a vast vertical pattern.

But a humble car-washer in Chicago recently conceived a brilliant yet simple variation on this idea.

Why not, he thought, lay them out *horizontally* instead of vertically, in other words, all side by side and build the necessary additional pylons to support them?

'Very clever,' sneered his foreman when he heard the idea. 'And what's the big idea?'

'I was coming to that. You could then use these parallel wires as the framework for a long platform made of vulcanite. Don't forget, vulcanite has two great qualities: it is a non-conductor of electricity and it makes a wonderful smooth, hard surface. So you could use the platform as a perfect overhead motorway!'

I need hardly tell you that when the foreman realised the brilliance of the humble car-washer's stroke of genius, he begged forgiveness for his rudeness and made him shake hands there and then, before taking him to meet the boss of the company. The boss realised, too, that the car-washer had stumbled on an idea which would make their fortune, and being an American businessman in the traditional mould tearfully clapped him on the shoulder and led him to his eldest daughter, saying:

'I was wrong to stand between you two young things; take her, boy, she's yours.'

Which surprised them both, as they had never met before in their lives.


## A FEW INGENIOUS IDEAS

Humorists may think themselves very funny when they invent things like water-proof curtains for submarines or tiny muzzles to stop snails dribbling on lettuce plants, but they cannot hold a candle to the genuine, serious inventor. Next time you have a moment to spare, go along to the Ministry of Commerce and take a look at the thousands of patents registered by inspired inventors every day; I guarantee you will be wreathed in smiles within five minutes, if not rocking with laughter.

Here are a few samples of inventors and their inventions, just to whet your appetite.

(I have copied everything down word for word. They are all genuine, believe me.)

*       *       *

Bastide, 20 December 1900: A device for retrieving the mustard left inside used mustard jars.

Tourigny, 14 December 1900: Ventilated shoes.

Paulsen, 25 January 1900: An electrical indicator to remind one of the arrival of break-time.

Argyle, 27 September 1898: An improved combination meerschaum pipe and police whistle.

Malet, 7 October 1898: A device for informing all motor car tourists of their exact position, difficulties ahead, local hazards and interesting attractions nearby.

De Salabert, 16 November 1898: A luminous hat.

Couturier, 18 January 1899: A method of converting motor cycles into four-wheeled vehicles.

Shea, 3 January 1899: A device for the use of ladies (?).

Potthof and Mme Buckel, 12 December 1898: A device for gathering up children's excrement.

Bichara Malhame, 9 May 1899: A scented calendar.

Dupoux, 25 November 1898: Completely new method, guaranteed sure and infallible, of manufacturing or preparing mayonnaise sauce.

Langrême, 26 November 1899: A power-assisted horse.

Girdelement, 13 October 1898: An improved pipe designed to give off more smoke.

Konig, 22 October: Footwear for animals.

Von Reinolts, 25 February 1900: Apparatus designed to play a variety of practical jokes.

Wulff, 25 April 1899: Method of teaching animals to play music.

Leps and Barda, 1 May 1899: A bus without brakes.

De Saint Jean, 1 April 1899: Combined fishing rod and bicycle pump.

Etc., etc., etc. . . .

I could go on for ever, but I won't.

## SOME MORE INGENIOUS IDEAS

The value of a standing ovation is not so much the value of the noise made by those standing up to applaud you, as the degree of respect you have for those who have stood up and the amount of time you have for their motives.

For only a fool would feel proud to be praised for virtues he did not possess.

. . . These musings, informed by a certain bitterness, are brought on by the reading of all those publications which rushed to reprint the list I gave last week of patients registered with the state.

As these inventions had a touch of the crackpot about them (despite my perfectly serious treatment of them) nobody felt like admitting that they might be completely authentic. So as one man the said publications showered compliments on me for my wonderful imagination, whereas I was nothing but a pale transcriber of the truth.

What will they say when they see the new list I have copied out for them without a single jot or comma changed (may the gods bear witness that I am telling the truth!)?

Here we go, then.

*     *     *

Viany-Allemand, 23 May 1899 – A parasol to keep off frost.

Samat-Roubaud and Debrien, 10 July 1899 – A revolving café-restaurant.

Bitter, 27 June 1900 – The Venus de Milo restored.

Lazarus, 19 July 1900 – A device to prevent the illegal use of tricycles.

Buczkowski, 18 July 1900 – A self-locking saucer.

Nau and Greiner, 8 September 1899 — An automatic device for immobilising and extinguishing cigars, candles, etc. . . .

Demaria, 18 August 1899 – A multi-coloured walking-stick.

Friedrich, 5 November 1900 – A bullet-proof haversack.

Green, 17 October 1899 – Shield for cyclists.

Letorey, 11 November 1899 – A balloon modified in order to execute internal or external alterations to a building.

De la Houssaye, 1 December 1899 – Sea-water soap.

Funck, 8 December 1899 – A combined brush and watering can.

Wenckheim, 3 May 1900 – Sweat-free spectacles.

Lindbohm, 28 December 1899 – Electrical fishing-rod.

Charaviber, 9 January 1900 – Combined salt cellar/cigar-holder.

Reimer, 19 February 1900 – Transparent automobile globe (???)

Rey, 21 February 1900 – Boat and oars made from cavalry lances, steel tubes and tent pegs.

Maubrey, 4 March 1900 – Pictorial cakes.

Mautner, 7 April 1900 – A device to keep the body upright during long train journeys.

Leroux, 12 April 1900 – An appliance for reducing over-large mouths and making thin lips bigger.

Bellamy, 23 April 1900 – Devices for aerial recreation.

Eisenmeyer, 24 April 1900 – A method of protecting parts of the body against atmospheric pressure.

Etc., etc., etc. . . .

*        *        *

One final note.

In case any of our readers should be seduced by the magnificence of this list into wishing to invest in any of the aforesaid inventions, we shall always be glad to act as agents, for the appropriate bloated fee.

# A THIRD AND FINAL BATCH OF INGENIOUS IDEAS

Furious protests, bitter-sweet reproaches, dignified remonstrations, prospectuses, tracts, brochures – good God! the avalanche on my elegant rosewood writing desk has been unending.

And all from inventors who wish to explain to me that their patents (which I recently listed in these pages) in no way deserve the description 'having a touch of the crackpot about them' which I invoked.

On the contrary! There have seldom been such deserving inventions in history as these (they are all unanimous in pointing to their own in particular) and if humanity should pass by on the other side, then the word 'progress' is a meaningless bisyllable, it seems.

Some of the inventors, like M. Ary Bitter (of Marseille), who had devised a reconstruction of the Venus de Milo, are in true despair at the lack of success attending their enterprise.

Others are concerned merely to correct my misconceptions.

Such as M. Charaviber, who writes to say:

'In your summary of imaginative patents published in *Le Journal* you were good enough to mention mine, number 296015, taken out on 9 January 1900. Unfortunately you mis-read "salière porte-cirage" for "salière porte-cigare". My invention is not a combined salt-cellar/cigar-holder; it is a combined salt-cellar/wax polish-holder.'

And why should anyone want anything so far-fetched?

The answer is simplicity itself.

With a view to persuading customers to buy the wax polish that *he* manufactures rather than a rival brand, M. Charaviber has had the astute idea of replacing the usual metal polish container with an elegant glass salt-cellar which can be used (when the wax is finished) on even the most fashionable dining table. After a quick wash, of course.

But we could spend all day on the information offered by these good men so, fascinating though it is, I shall now with your permission, ladies and gentlemen, proceed to complete this study of contemporary ingenuity with a third and last list of patents. All guaranteed absolutely genuine. (Anyone can check them.)

\*        \*        \*

Chapoulart, Pouzioux and Bucher, 13 January 1900 – A theatrical entertainment on rails.

Garnier, 1 February 1901 – Spare metal legs for wooden horses.

Konig Co Ltd, 26 September 1898 – Apparatus to enable readers to find any passage in any book at great speed.

Barth, 12 October 1898 – Improved device for the successive pivoting of a certain number of arms on the same axis (?).

Julie, 16 June 1899 – Apparatus for castrating animals.

Béguin, 21 June 1900 – Free supply of addresses. (??)

Martin, 18 July 1900 – Device for preventing coastlines from being eroded by the sea.

Hoover and Hoover, 22 September 1899–Contraption for harvesting plums.

Rubak, 2 October 1899 – A summer fez.

Mini, 18 October 1900 – Apparatus for reading a book behind glass without having to touch the page.

Launier, 16 Novemeber 1900 – Mobile articulated copper stair-case.

Morel, 9 October 1900 – Restaurant with mobile tables.

Franck, 23 October 1899 – Articulated figurine for use either as a tooth-pick or an ear-pick.

Mlle Thornton, 20 November 1899 – Accessory to be fitted to one's belt for holding an umbrella over one's head.

Etc., etc., etc. . . .

\*        \*        \*

I hope you agree with me that this material is every bit as thought-provoking as it is entertaining.


# THE PREVENTION OF CRUELTY
# TO MICROBES

I went into the humble crémerie where I come for my breakfast every day. I sat down next to a tall fair young man who seemed totally harmless, not to say ineffectual. I politely asked the waiter for my usual two boiled eggs. And then, quite without warning, the young man rose to his feet and fired a revolver at my heart.

Luckily, either his pistol was of an inferior make or he was using second-hand ammunition, because instead of burying itself in me his bullet bounced off my side (I have iron sides) and left me with nothing much worse than extensive contusions.

Still, when I saw that I was actually bleeding I thought it best not to waste time in idle recriminations but to hie me straightaway to the nearest apothecary.

To whom I must pay public tribute at this point for the selfless way in which he dropped everything to staunch my wound, while at the same time recording my deep distress at his ability to make puns at such a tragic moment. At every available opportunity he said, over and over again:

'I take after Descartes, you know. *Je panse, donc j'essuie.*'

My would-be assassin, meanwhile, the tall fair young man who had seemed so harmless not to say ineffectual, had followed me all the way to the chemist's and was busy helping him with the bandaging and the dressing. So when the operation was over, the killer and I made our way back to the crémerie and tucked into breakfast with the best verve in the world, for, as you can imagine, all that hard work had left us ravenous.

'Now,' I asked the young man, 'will you not tell me what drove you to this desperate act of violence?'

'Gladly. You know how that idiot chemist claimed just now to take after Descartes? Well, *I* take after the Swedish student who shot a toreador the other day because he loved animals so much.'

'I don't quite see . . .'

'It was because I heard you ordering two boiled eggs. I just couldn't help myself . . . but you know what happened next.'

'Yes, agreed, but . . . I mean, I know that eggs are of animal origin. That doesn't mean they have any feeling, though.'

'Quite so. It's not the eggs I feel sorry for. It's the millions of little microscopic organisms, ultra-microscopic even, which swim around in water so innocently and happily even though we can't see them. You see, if you suddenly raise the temperature of their native element, it produces a heat which they are quite untrained for and which has dire effects on them. And you can't boil eggs without boiling water.'

'You could be right.'

'Of course I'm right. Now, taking pity on the sufferings of a bull is all very good and proper. But, sir, one bull is only one bull, whereas when you prepare something even as small as a cup of camomile tea you cause more agony and more suffering than has been produced in all the bull rings of the world in the last few centuries.'

'By God! What a terrible thought. But is there nothing we can do about it?'

'Yes, certainly. It's quite simple. Whenever you absolutely *have* to boil some water, just put a good helping of cocaine in it. Because cocaine removes all sense of feeling from microbes.'

*          *          *

I have followed the young man's advice ever since. Which explains why all those who have done me the honour of dining at my house recently have thought the cooking tasted decidedly odd and gone home feeling wretchedly ill for no apparent reason.

# THE PAPER CRISIS

You may have noticed that I have spent most of my recent waking life writing distraught articles about the imminent disappearance of the world's trees, brought about by our insatiable demand for more and more paper. You may have wondered at the time if there was some special reason for my new obsession. You may even have suspected that I had a hidden commercial interest.

Well, of course I had! I might as well tell you now – before you think of the idea yourself – that I have already set up a little public company which, if it achieves nothing else, will cause a world-wide sensation and make a vast fortune for me. And for you, if you are wise enough to buy shares in it.

Personally, I feel that it will appeal most of all to those small savers and investors who have been so badly treated recently, but it is also bound to be highly attractive to the big investor and no less so to the medium-sized investor. If on the other hand you have no savings of any shape or size, it makes no difference; just get hold of some money and make it available to me.

The main purpose of my new company, I need hardly say, is eminently progressive and ecological. Briefly, we intend *to do without paper wherever it is not absolutely necessary* and instead to use only substances discovered by modern science.

There are some pundits who claim that we are now living in a Golden Age of Paper. I disagree. My counter-argument runs roughly as follows: You stupid, cretinous imbeciles, you haven't the faintest idea what you're talking about! Why, our grand-children will think paper to be no more sophisticated than we now consider prehistoric flint. Golden Age of Paper, indeed!

No, no, my friends and fellow shareholders-to-be, let us abandon this sad, sad fallacy.

Not that I advocate for one moment doing away with news-papers or magazines or books.

On the contrary, I pray that the freedom of the press may shine ever more brightly in our society.

May truth, justice and beauty roll forth ever more dazzling in the fearless editorials of this great land of ours!

May . . .!

But back to business.

I cannot emphasise too strongly that my little company has been formed primarily to ensure that our dailies, weeklies, monthlies, yearlies and other publications no longer depend on paper. And if there be any person so trapped in the archaic world of printing and publishing (especially publishing) that he cannot conceive of an alternative to paper, now is the time for him to be enlightened.

Newspapers *can* survive without paper!

Magazines *can* be printed without paper!

Novels *can* be read without paper!

Let me tell you how.

To start with, my new company will devote most of its resources to publishing every day, if not more often, a new periodical called *The Daily Celluloid*. All subscribers to this new daily (which will, incidentally, be the best written and most informative of all time) will receive with the first issue a small machine reminiscent of a magic lantern, though not nearly so complicated. You will also get a booklet containing the few instructions needed to work it.

And you will receive, every day, a copy of *The Daily Celluloid*, which is a small transparent rectangle about the size of a playing card. All you have to do is insert it into a slot in the machine and project on your wall the best selection of news from French papers and from foreign dailies as well.

This miracle is made possible simply by micro-photographing eight or ten pages of a large master newspaper and transferring the results onto the small card mentioned in the last paragraph.

As soon as I have established this enterprise on a firm footing, I shall examine other ways in which the new process can provide us with fat profits, or confer benefits on society or simply enable us to find new ways of shocking the French bourgeoisie.

Meanwhile, send in your subscription as soon as possible.

Although I am very busy with many other projects at the moment, I shall personally welcome all funds sent in by potential shareholders.

Don't forget – to avoid disappointment, send me your money *now*.

# COMMERCIAL INTERLUDE

(Scene: an ironmonger's shop. The door opens and a customer comes in.)

* * *

*Customer*: Good morning.

*Ironmonger*: Good morning, sir. Can I help you?

*Customer*: Yes. I'm looking for one of those gadgets which you fix on a door so that it closes by itself, with a spring. If you know what I mean.

*Ironmonger*: An automatic door-closer?

*Customer*: That's it! An automatic door-closer. Not too expensive, if possible.

*Ironmonger*: One medium-price automatic door-closer, then.

*Customer*: That's right. As long as it's not too complicated and fiddly.

*Ironmonger*: Of course not, sir. Just a cheap, simple automatic door-closer.

*Customer*: Yes, please. But I don't want one of those really strong ones that pull the door shut before you're halfway through . . .

*Ironmonger*: . . . and tear half your jacket off? I know the kind you mean! No, no, what you need is a simple, reasonably priced automatic door-closer, with gentle action. Does that cover it?

*Customer*: Absolutely. Not *too* gentle, though. I've seen some door-closers that work so slowly . . .

*Ironmonger*: . . . the door's still half open next time you come back? Right! Don't tell me! What *you're* looking for is a simple budget model, gentle-action quick return door-closer.

*Customer*: I think that covers everything. As long as it isn't too stiff. One or two makes seem to be so powerful that you have to push like mad to get the door open at all.

*Ironmonger*: Right. So what we're after is a low cost, straight-for-ward, gentle-action, quick return, easy-to-operate automatic door-closer.

*Customer*: That's it. Could I have a look at what you've got, please?

*Ironmonger*: Sorry, sir. Don't do door-closers, sir.

# FAMILY LIFE

Ribeyrou and Delavanne, two inseparable friends, had spent their entire Sunday afternoon in the Latin Quarter passing from one big café to another and visiting all the bars where the girls were, scrupulously careful not to miss a single one out.

Until shortly before seven they abruptly remembered that they had been invited out to dinner somewhere in the boulevard de Clichy.

Luckily, the Place Pigalle bus came past and stopped, welcoming them open-armed. They got in and sat down, rather touched by its solicitude.

You should know, by the way, that the route they were about to embark on takes in the Quai des Orfèvres. A curious street, the Quai des Orfèvres. The houses all follow the same pattern; a little shop on the ground floor and then, above shop level, a tiny mezzanine apartment looking more like a ship's cabin than anything on dry land.

And as the shops themselves are not very tall, the tops of the buses are on the same level as the mezzanine (always assuming the wheel-base of the bus is at road level) and the passengers can see into the mezzanine apartment with amazing ease.

The same applied, of course, to Ribeyrou and Delavanne. So when a traffic jam brought their bus to a complete halt for a minute or more, they found themselves, willy-nilly, party to a little family gathering.

The shop they had stopped in front of belonged to a heraldic engraver or armorial block-maker.

Upstairs they could see the whole family sitting ready for the evening meal round the table, and on the table an appetising, steaming tureen of soup.

There was father, and mother, and two grown-up daughters about twenty years old (wearing matching dresses) and another daughter, much younger.

The weather being fine and warm that evening, these nice people had left their window wide open.

And the bus being so close, everyone on board could smell the delicious fragrance of the family stock-pot.

Ribeyrou and Delavanne were completely mesmerised by

the domestic tableau. They both felt a lump come into their throat.

Then the bus set off again.

Delavanne was the first to break the silence.

'There's real family life for you.'

'It must be a wonderful life,' said Ribeyrou.

'Far better than the kind of life we lead.'

'Much more restful, too.'

'I wouldn't mind taking another look at those nice people. Come on – let's get off and go back!'

Unfortunately, there wasn't much to see from street level. The circle of light on the ceiling from the table lamp, and that was about it.

So they went all the way back to the Place Saint-Michel, had a quick absinthe (one for the road), and climbed on to another bus which was just leaving. This time the traffic was flowing freely. The mezzanine apartment looked as appealing as ever but it went past far too fast.

They just got a glimpse of mother serving roast beef. Or was it? There wasn't really time to be sure.

'Ah, family life!' said Ribeyrou again, with a sigh.

'Tell you what it reminds me of, it reminds me of those Dutch interiors by . . . that painter . . . know the one?'

'Yes, I know the one you mean . . . the Flemish artist . . . .'

'That's the one!'

'Shall we have another look.'

'Suits me.'

So the whole performance took place again, not once but ten times, each circuit being punctuated by an absinthe (one for the road) in the Place Saint-Michel.

The bus station staff began to get worried about their strange behaviour. But as the travellers were otherwise just as orderly as the other passengers, there seemed to be no cause for interference.

They simply got on the bus, had their look, got off, walked back and got on the next bus . . . .

Meanwhile the heraldic engraver and his family were quietly getting on with their meal, totally unaware that its progress was being surveyed with great emotion by two young men on a bus.

The beef was followed by a leg of lamb, followed by haricot beans, then a salad, then dessert.

Presently the evening became a little cooler and they shut the windows.

One of the daughters sat down at the piano. Another could be seen singing.

From their vantage in the bus they could hear nothing but they knew instinctively that the music must be delightful.

After the absorption of so many absinthes (about a dozen for the road) the two friends had become very powerfully affected by their experience. They were now crying openly, like babies.

'Ah! Family life! Ah!'

Till brusquely Delavanne came to a momentous decision.

'Look! We're being stupid making ourselves unhappy like this. The solution is in our own hands, dammit! All we have to do is go and knock on their door *and ask for the two daughters' hands in marriage*! Right?'

So they did.

You can imagine the kind of reception they got.

The heraldic engraver was dumb-struck. Not for long though – once recovered, he delivered a short speech of amazing pungency in which the phrase 'drunken oafs!' recurred with regrettable frequency.

Delavanne showed admirable dignity in retreat.

'My dear proletarian sir, you are perfectly entitled to refuse our kind offer if you wish, but your speech of refusal would have lost nothing by being couched in more select language.'

'Oh, come on!' said Ribeyrou. 'We have to get to Montmartre. Let's catch the bus.'

'Bus? Not for me, thanks. I've seen enough buses for one day.'

And it came to pass the next morning, after a wild night on the tiles, that the two friends found themselves near the Bastion de Saint-Ouen, without having the faintest recollection of the chain of events that had brought them to such an outlandish part of Paris.

They took refuge in a nearby café and ordered a cognac-and-cassis each (one for the road). Midway through, Delavanne suddenly burst into helpless laughter.

'Don't tell me,' said Ribeyrou. 'You're thinking of the heraldic engraver and his family.'

'Yes! Sitting up there 'tween decks . . . .'

'Can you imagine . . .?'

'What cretins . . .!'

And they both went off home to bed.

# SENSITIVITY

I am taking the plunge at last, ladies and gentlemen. I am getting married!

More fool you, I hear my readers cry.

And you're absolutely right. I couldn't agree more. More fool me.

I'm getting married all the same.

Wait till you hear who I'm getting married to, though. Then you'll really be up in arms. Not to a woman like that, you'll say, not to one of those, surely you can't seriously mean you're going to marry a . . .?

Yes, I can and to prove it I am. And let me tell you something else – any reader who had found himself in the same position as me would have felt exactly the same way I did and ended up marrying her just as I am. So no more idle criticism, please.

Thank you.

Not that it's my fault anyway. Personally, I blame the mud.

Funny stuff, Paris mud.

Country mud I can understand. The country can't help being full of mud. When the rain comes down it mixes with the soil and what have you got? You've got mud.

But Paris is different. How can rain mix with paving stones or asphalt? Exactly. So where does all the mud in Paris come from?

The day I become a millionaire (the event is tentatively scheduled for the middle of next month) I shall immediately institute an award of 350,000 francs to be given to the best essay on 'Paris Mud Through the Ages'. No, make that 'Paris *Muds* Through the Ages'. Because there are as many different kinds of mud in our capital as there are streets. Go out into Paris on a rainy day, wander from district to district, and before your very feet you'll see stiff mud, runny mud, black mud, grey mud – every kind of mud. I have even seen bright purple mud. (Only in Impressionist paintings, admittedly.)

But the most aristocratic mud to be found anywhere in Paris, a mud which I can recommend personally after extensive tests, is the mud to be found in the rue des Martyrs. Smooth? It's so smooth it's like cold cream in mourning. So bland is it, so soothing, so oily, so *mellifluous* is it, that any doctor could safely prescribe it as an ointment for a lady's chapped breast.

To look at it reminds me of a darker version of dubbin.

Did they use dubbin in your regiment when you were in the army?

I was in the 119th Regt, and if you were in the ranks like me you had to put dubbin on your boots once a week.

At least.

There was nothing, absolutely nothing like dubbin for keeping leather fresh and supple, they said – our captain even claimed the stuff gave the leather something to feed on.

Feed on, I ask you!

The worst bit was trying to shine your boots the day after you'd fed the brutes.

Which reminds me – I still laugh every time I think of it – of an excellent practical joke I once played, with the help of dubbin, on a new recruit to the regiment.

The very first day he joined I spotted him in the mess hall chewing his rations in a half-hearted sort of way, so I went over to cheer him up.

'Eat up, lad,' I said. 'Can't have you losing your appetite, you know.'

'It's not that – it's just that I don't fancy this beef very much.'

'Well, why not have some mustard? That'll help it down a bit.'

'Not a bad idea. Where do they keep the mustard round here?'

I helpfully fetched a jar of dubbin and invited him to get stuck in.

All unsuspecting, the poor lad took a good helping on his mess tin lid and dipped every mouthful of meat in it.

Laugh? I almost died.

He went one better. His system revolted against the meat-and-dubbin mixture and he brought it all up again, but in his convulsions he must have injured some vital internal organ because that very night he was admitted to the military hospital and died before dawn.*

I've never had such a good laugh in all my life.

\*          \*          \*

As I was saying, oiliness is a quality much prized in cold cream and in religion (ever noticed how the top priests are always the oiliest?), but for sheer unctuous blandness nobody can touch the

---

*An interesting demonstration of the fact that swallowing a non-toxic substance can sometimes lead to death.

mud in the rue des Martyrs.

Without falling over.

Which is where we came in.

I was walking back home the other night after a day of rain, and the ground had become so treacherous that the passers-by had to fight as hard to keep their balance as if they were sailors inching along a bowsprit covered in olive oil.

I managed to keep my vertical axis perpendicular to the centre of the earth as far as the Café des Martyrs, but there my feet finally slipped from beneath me and I fell flat on my pavement.

I was absolutely covered in the stuff, also in confusion, shame and humiliation (none of it helped much by the laughter of the friendly onlookers).

I was just picking myself up when I felt a helping hand on my shoulder and turned round to find that it belonged to a rather nice-looking fair-haired girl. She smiled at me and said:

'Never mind, come over to my place and you can get cleaned up there.'

She lived just across the road, it turned out.

Well, at a time like that you don't try to take advantage of the situation, you just go along with it. So I went along.

And a few minutes later she was busy helping me out of my outer clothing, wiping the dirt off and brushing them all down in a maternal sort of way, before returning them to me in their pristine condition.

While she was thus engaged, I had plenty of time to take a good look round her quarters and I suddenly realised that my benefactress was nothing other than a lady of the streets.

Well, I had to show her my gratitude somehow. So why not by offering her my custom there and then?

But when I did, she gently edged away from me and whispered: 'No, don't, I'd rather you didn't.'

'Why not, for heaven's sake?'

'Because . . .'

'Because *what* . . .?'

'Well, because then you'd only think I'd helped you so that I could get you back here and take advantage of you.'

The idea was ludicrous, but nothing I said could make her change her mind.

I wouldn't have minded so much, except that she really was an extraordinarily attractive girl.

So I came back the next day, clean and dry.

Still no good.

Resisting adamantly, she said: 'I'm sorry, I couldn't possibly. I know what you'd say. You'd say I only came to your rescue because I was after your business. I'm sorry, but no.'

'Honestly,' I said, 'I wouldn't say anything of the sort. Honestly I wouldn't.'

'You might not say it, but you'd be sure to think it.'

Well, I have been going back to her every day and not once have I managed to wring the slightest concession out of her.

How could one possibly not fall in love with a nature of such sensitivity?

So now you know why I have asked her to be the mother of my children.

## THE GOOD PAINTER

Tonal harmony was his passion in life. The sight of clashing colours made him gnash his teeth as furiously as violent discords would a musician. In the provinces he was upset by the clashing ensembles of ladies' costumes; at the Paris Opera by the clashing costumes of ladies' ensembles.

It was such an obsession that whenever he ate fried eggs he never drank red wine at the same meal, for fear of the vile colour scheme it would produce in his stomach.

Once, hurrying along the pavement, he happened to bump into a flashy young man wearing a fawn overcoat and knock him against a freshly decorated shop-front (WET PAINT – DO NOT TOUCH).

'You might look where you're going!' protested the young man.

The artist stood back and squinted at him in the manner of painters studying their work.

'I don't see what you've got to complain about,' he said. 'The effect is very . . . Japanese.'

Not long ago he received a letter from an old friend of his who was out in Java hunting black panthers for the Wild Animal Stores of Trieste. Touched at the thought of someone so far away and so long ago remembering him, he wrote a long letter back to his old friend and packed it up in a huge envelope. Java being very distant and the letter being very heavy, the postage cost him a small fortune.

The Post Office clerk grumpily dished out six or seven stamps of varying hue and price.

Taking infinite pains, the artist proceeded to stick the stamps on the big envelope in a vertical row making sure that all the colours were in exactly the right combination. (There's nothing worse than a loud letter.)

More or less satisfied, he was about to thrust it into the gaping void marked ABROAD when a last look at the stamps caused him to return abruptly to the counter.

'A three sou stamp, please.'

'Certainly, sir.'

And he stuck it on the envelope below all the others.

'If I may say so, sir,' said the employee, unbending a little, 'the letter was quite correctly stamped already.'

'I know that, thank you,' said the artist obligingly. 'I needed a blue highlight.'

# PERSONAL COLUMN

*To Madame la Marquise de Ch.* . . . Please return your last shipment of prussic acid to us. If it really is corked, as you say, we shall of course replace it free of charge.

\*　　　\*　　　\*

*To M.V.P.* – Well, it's your own fault. If you hadn't tried to impress your doctor by telling him you were a solicitor, instead of admitting that you really worked as a fire-eater in a travelling circus, then Dr. Pelet (who is an extremely conscientious physician) would not have given you nitro-glycerine tablets to take, and you would not consequently have suffered from internal explosions, burnings and mild indigestion. That will teach you to bluff your way through life, dear boy.

\*　　　\*　　　\*

*To the Marquise de B.* . . . No, you won't find any more edible oysters now till September, except in really exclusive shops. The best month for eating oysters, of course, is February which has no less than two r's in it.

\*　　　\*　　　\*

*To the brothers Rothschild* – No problem at all. Drop in and borrow 100 sous any time you like.

*          *          *

*To H.M. Queen Victoria* – There is no excuse at all for your confusion. One is spelled Bauer, the other Boer. Don't you ever read the papers?

*          *          *

*To Mme Q. Hyer, of Pau* – Well, I went to the boulevard des Capucines and looked for the number you mentioned, but I couldn't find a field of rape anywhere. Are you sure you got the address right?

*          *          *

*To Mademoiselle Nina Pack of the Opéra Comique* – Your letter is charming, mademoiselle, but your anthropology leaves a little to be desired. If a man is of average height it does not necessarily follow that he is the product of a giant father and dwarf mother.

*          *          *

*To Mmes Jane à Digne* (*Basses–Alpes*) *and Jane à Ding* (*c/o navigable section of the Upper Mekong River*) – I have used the following method for many years and always found it worked perfectly.

First, I heat the water to boiling point. Then without warning I put it out in a draught. Microbes, you are doubtless aware, have a very weak chest and this brings on a bad chill from which they scarcely recover.

When I find it too troublesome to build a fire – if I am out bicycling, for instance, or stranded on pack-ice – I make do by spiking the water with a little gin (1 part water to 3 parts gin).

This latter method was given to me personally by Captain Cap and is just as good.

*          *          *

*To M. Michesse* (*of the firm Michesse et Rieux*) – I agree, the anomaly you mention is certainly extremely odd, but I can think of an even odder one. Did you know that the word 'cage' is masculine in the country, but feminine in town?

So, for instance, one says 'L'oiseau chante dans le bocage' in the country, but in town one would say 'L'oiseau chante dans la belle cage'.

I can see now why foreigners have difficulty learning French.

*          *          *

April 26 1896

*To Paul Escudier, Town Councillor of Paris* – Many thanks for your 30 francs, which I have already spent. In all honesty, I should tell you that I no longer reside in the Saint-Georges district and therefore cannot vote for you.

My local councillor is now M. Bompard, to whom I have already pledged my vote. I am sure he will be glad to reimburse you.

\*          \*          \*

April 29 1896

*To Messrs. Puglesi-Conti and Urbain Gohier* – Very well, gentlemen, I shall vote for you as well.

\*          \*          \*

*To Léon Gandillot, Paris* – You have been correctly informed, sir. Cats that eat flies never get fat.

The same applies to tigers. Especially if they eat nothing but flies.

\*          \*          \*

*To Captain Ch. Lamy, on board Destroyer 166* – To find the time of the spring neap tide, simply add thirty-six hours to the date of the equinox. The height of the neap tide in any port is the product of the height above sea level of the port *times* a hundredth of the tide level *plus* the normal tide.

See you soon, I hope.

\*          \*          \*

May I remind all readers wishing to write to me to enclose a 15 centime stamp? Not for the reply – I never reply to readers' letters – but to help pay for my correspondence with tradesmen.

\*          \*          \*

## NEWS IN BRIEF

Instead of persecuting bookmakers and innocent flower-girls, the Chief of Police would be far better employed controlling the hordes of bicycles which are causing such a nuisance in this hot weather. Only yesterday morning a bicycle escaped from its shed in the rue Vivienne and rushed at top speed down the street, knocking into all the passers by and leaving a trail of terror and consternation in its wake. It got as far as the junction of the boulevard Montparnasse and the rue Lepic before a brave gendarme managed to bring it down with a bullet in its left pedal.

The autopsy showed that it had gone certifiably mad.

A hand-cart which it bit en route is still under day-and-night observation at the Pasteur Institute.

*          *          *

*To M. Franc-Nohain of La Rochelle:* The case you report is not as unusual as you think. I have noticed that adulterous wives frequently marry cuckolded husbands.

*          *          *

*To the Marquise de F. . . of Blois:* Yes, madame, you are absolutely right: the gentleman in question was indeed myself. I was not nearly as drunk as you make out, though.

# A TACTICAL ERROR

One fine morning the river ferry steamed across from Le Havre to Honfleur as it always did, and deposited on the Honfleur quayside an impressively unusual figure. He was a grizzled old seaman, obviously as hard as a ton of nails, tough as old beef, and so tanned by sun and rain that the children on the quay took him at first for a negro, till they looked closer. The kind of man you or I would expect to go straight about his business with no nonsense or hanging about.

You or I would be quite wrong, because the first thing he did was stroll over to the seawall, drop his large canvas bag in the dust and take a good, long look at the town, as if the whole place belonged to him and he had nothing better to do than stand and stare at it.

'Blow me, but nothing much has changed,' he muttered, after a while. 'The Harbour Master's place is still just the same. The White Horse Hotel. And old Deliquaire's shop. And the old town hall. They've rebuilt St. Catherine's, though. Not before time, neither.'

But when he started looking at the people round him, it was a different story. He didn't recognise a single one of them.

Which wasn't really too surprising, considering it was his first visit to the place in thirty years or more.

What was surprising, perhaps, was that someone suddenly hove into view whom the sailor did recognise, a white-haired old officer with a couple of medals stuck on his jacket and a big cigar stuck in his mouth. As soon as the old seaman spotted him, he told a young lad to look after his bag for a moment and then approached the man respectfully, taking off his cap as he addressed him.

'Morning, Cap'n Forestier, and I trust things are well with you, sir. Do you remember me by any chance? No, I can see as you don't. It's Théophile Vincent, sir. I worked with you on the *Fair Ida* once. Down Valparaiso way.'

The captain looked closely at him.

'Good God! Old Théophile! Well, I'll be damned. I thought you'd gone down to Davy Jones's locker long ago.'

'No, Cap'n, not by a long chalk. That's one gentleman I've no immediate plans for getting acquainted with.'

While the two old mariners started chewing over old times, a couple of veteran local pilots drifted over out of curiosity, followed by an odd longshoreman or two, and one by one they all recognised Théophile. He gave them his news as briefly as he could, then started to ask after old friends.

'What happened to So-and-so?'

'Dead, I'm afraid.'

'Ah. What about So-and-so?'

'Lost at sea.'

'Well, what about What's-his-name?'

'He never came back. No-one ever found out what happened to him.'

After which he got round to inquiring about the fate of his own relations, only to be told that almost all of them had gone down to whoever looks after the land-lubbers' locker.

It turned out that the only family he had left in the whole wide world consisted of two nieces, one of whom had got married to the local bailiff, the other ending up as a farmer's wife not far from Honfleur.

Logically, Théophile decided to go and look up the bailiff first. He had no qualms left about invading the privacy of officialdom, not after thirty years spent knocking about the South Seas, so he picked up his bag, said goodbye to his rediscovered friends and didn't stop walking till he was standing in the middle of the bailiff's office.

The only person in the bailiff's office, however, was a young office boy engaged in the vital task of transforming a page of dull regulations into a passable drawing of a whaling launch. Théophile

cast his eye over the sketch, gave the lad the benefit of his knowledge of the construction of launches in general and of whalers in
particular till the drawing was improved out of all recognition,
and finally got round to asking:

'Where can I find Irma?'

'Irma?' said the lad, nonplussed.

'Yes. The bailiff's wife. She's my niece.'

'Ah. He's gone home for lunch.'

Five minutes later Théophile burst unceremoniously into his
niece's dining room, just as the family were sitting down to their
midday meal.

'Morning, Irma, and good morning to you too, sir! By God,
Irma, I says it as maybe shouldn't, but you've changed a hell of a
lot in thirty years! You were all peaches and cream last time I saw
you. You look more like an old guava now!'

Irma's husband took this in quite the wrong spirit, I'm afraid,
and went scarlet with rage. He was not a nice sort at all – an
unlovable, bad-tempered red-head as well as being one of those
petty civil servants whose fat behinds seem created expressly to
invite the shotgun pellets of the resentful poor.

Irma sided with him, sad to say.

In other words. Théophile got such short shrift that within
seconds he had humped his bag on his shoulder again and was on
his way back to the harbour. He ended up in a sailors' tavern
where he ate, drank and stood countless round to such good effect
that he ended up just that little bit intoxicated. So it wasn't until
the evening that he remembered he still had another niece to see;
Constance. She's a country lass, he thought to himself. *She'll* lay
on the hospitality, anyway.

Constance and family were hard at work on the evening stew
when he arrived.

'Bon appétit, everyone!' he cried, as he entered.

Constance got up, looking very hard and cold.

'And what might *you* be after?'

'Constance! Don't you recognise me, old girl?'

'Never seen you before in my life.'

'But I'm your uncle Théophile!'

'Rubbish. He's dead.'

'No, he's not! And here I am to prove it!'

'That's as may be. But he's dead as far as we're concerned.
Understand? Now clear off.'

Théophile understood. He also conveyed, in a few short, sharp, spicy expressions, exactly what he thought of her and her poxy family. Then he wandered off into the night again, not without a certain sadness though, which he proceeded to assuage very thoroughly back in the sailors' tavern in the company of his old mates from sea-faring days. The treatment proved so effective that by the time the police came to close the place down at eleven, everyone present was crying tears of pure gin at the thought of the decline of the world of sail. So much so that they all sallied forth with the firm intention of rowing out to scuttle a large Norwegian steamer that lay at anchor in the harbour waiting for the tide.

Needless to say, nothing was scuttled by anyone and they all reached their beds with no harm done.

When Théophile got up the next morning, his first important errand was to his lawyer, to whom he imparted the information that he was not just an old sailor back from a life on the ocean wave, he was also by way of being extremely rich. Because in that canvas bag there were no less than 200,000 francs, acquired in various dubious ways no doubt, but acquired nonetheless.

And it wasn't very long before the news of his opulence reached his nieces' ears, with startling results.

'My *dear* Uncle Théophile,' said Irma, 'if there is *ever* anything we can do . . . .'

'You must have thought us terribly rude,' said Constance, 'but I never *dreamt* that it was really you . . . .'

Théophile's reaction to these fervent protestations of love and affection could best be described as tending to the cynical. But as they seemed to be as undying as they were fervent, he eventually put an end to the family persecution by announcing that he would give both sides extreme pleasure by agreeing to stay six months of the year with one niece and the other six months with the other. And he further decreed that every Sunday both families should be together for a communal meal of great harmony and cordiality.

It was at one of these uneasy family get-togethers that Théophile made the following little speech:

'I need hardly remind you that we none of us know when we are likely to die . . . .'

All ears were pricked . . . .

'. . . So I have been and gone and made my will.'

Cries of protest and dismay.

'Yes, I have. And as, furthermore, I don't like the idea of splitting my fortune in two, I have decided to leave it all to one party.'

Muted chorus of consternation and dismay.

'No, I have made up my mind. I have decided to leave *all* my fortune . . . to . . . to whichever niece I am not staying with at the time of my death. So, for example, if I'm staying with you when I die, Irma, then all the money goes to Constance. And if I peg out at Constance's, Irma gets all the lolly. And so on, vice versa.'

It was a terrible dilemma in which the two families found themselves. Should they be pleased by this new arrangement? Or should they, on the other hand, be horrified by the whole idea? After vacillating a little while between horror and pleasure, they decided eventually to welcome the idea, each family having convinced itself that with a bit of luck and a lot of care it could easily win the uncle who laid the golden egg.

The said uncle was staying with Constance at the time, it being mid-summer and he being anxious to enjoy life in the country. And the way he was looked after, following that eventful Sunday lunch, would have made the average goose being stuffed for pâté de foie gras feel underprivileged. He had never been so pampered in all his life. Nor, come to that, had he ever chuckled to himself so much. But what he most enjoyed, curiously enough, was seeing his stomach grow round and contented. All his life he had poured scorn on the guzzlers and gourmands, on those who ate for sheer pleasure, but now he took a great sensual delight in the idea of having a nice little paunch of his own, with a gold chain and lots of trinkets to hang over it.

Then at last the summer ended. The rain returned, the air grew cold and it was time to take up winter quarters with Irma. But when he came to town and settled down in her house, he found there were other delights to make up for past rural pleasures. Women! Sliding into a new pattern of life, Théophile began to be late for meals. Sometimes he was not only late for meals, he missed them altogether. Once or twice, if the truth be known, he stayed out all night.

Not unnaturally, Irma began to get worried about her uncle's welfare and endurance. However, as she was amply endowed with that admirable intuition that God has seen fit to bestow on woman alone, she had the very good sense to deal with Uncle Théophile's problem by introducing into the household a new young maid, who was not only personally attractive but far from prudish in her outlook.

A splendid idea.

Not foolproof unfortunately, though.

Because within three months Théophile got married to the attractive and far from prudish maid, and changed his will accordingly.

# SPEED READING

Although I have been on the board of directors of the *Compagnie des Chemins de Fer de l'Ouest* since 1863, this month's meeting was the most interesting I have attended in all that time. And as we took several decisions which will alter the entire future of railway travel, I think you should be the first to hear about them.

One, reached after hours of passionate and heated argument, was to extend to Italian-speaking travellers the same facilities we laid on for English travellers a few months ago. I'm sure you know that when the Great Exhibition opened at that time, we made a radical alteration to the telegraph office at the Gare St. Lazare. Hitherto, the only indication of the nature of its business had been a large sign reading 'Télégraphe', but so as not to leave our cross-Channel visitors in any doubt whatsoever we took the big decision to add another sign reading 'Telegraph'.* Well, if we can do as much for the English it is only right and proper we do the same for the Italians, so very soon you will see a third sign, unmistakably saying 'Telegrafo'.

It is by little touches like these that the essential big-heartedness of a large railway company is known.

*   *   *

In passing, let me draw the attention of the Exhibition staff to the courtesy invariably shown by the officials of our railway company. They would never sink to the depths plumbed by one parasite of the Great Exhibition whom I encountered recently. I was walking across the Place de la Concorde when this street ticket-seller came up and shouted in my ear (there must be many Parisians who have gone deaf since the Exhibition started):

'Exhibition tickets, only eleven sous! Tickets eleven sous each! Get your tickets now!'

As I showed no interest in his clumsy advances he assumed I must be English, moved to my other ear and roared:

'Sixpence! Tickets, sixpence!'

So I turned to him and said severely:

'You rogue! Sixpence is nearly twenty sous. Why do you charge

* Absolutely true historical fact.

your fellow Frenchmen eleven sous, and foreigners almost twice that?'

'Ah, well, you see,' he said with engaging honesty, 'that's because I don't know the English for eleven sous.'

\*     \*     \*

But back to railways, and to our big policy decision.

For some years now the railway lines of France have been lined with vast hoardings leased out by the rail companies to various manufacturers, who have promptly taken advantage of these empty spaces to make shameless claims for their own products. This unattractive orgy of publicity has irritated many travellers, so much so that some of them would now rather stay at home than face the sight. Result: a drop in railway revenue and a loss of public sympathy.

So at last we have decided to do something about it.

In future, instead of those dreary advertising messages, we shall install one long continuous stretch of fencing on which we shall print highly entertaining and absorbing novels which can be read by train passengers as they speed past. At last the expression 'to race through a book' will become living reality. Everything will be done to ensure complete satisfaction; the books will be chosen by a panel of experts, the text will be printed in large legible type, the illustrations will be by leading painters of the day and so on.

They may be only one-line novels, but a line such as Gutenberg never dreamt of, stretching from Paris to the remotest railway terminus.

A few timid shareholders may object to the expense of the scheme. If so, they have nothing to fear. The novels we choose will be so enthralling that many travellers coming from, for instance, Marseille to Paris, will travel on to Le Havre far out of their way simply to find out if beautiful Blanche finally marries the handsome Vicomte, or if the wicked marquis meets with the fate he so richly deserves.

And the railway will be profitable again.

# POST OFFICE LOVE

When I got out of the train at Baisemoy-en-Cort the first thing I saw was the dog-cart belonging to my old friend Lenfileur, who had invited me down for the week.

And the first thing I asked him to do was take me to the local post office, because while in the train I had suddenly remembered something I had faithfully promised I would do before I left Paris and which shamefully, very shamefully, I had not done. Never mind what.

Baisemoy-en-Cort Post Office turned out to be notable chiefly for an air of austerity which could easily have tumbled any moment over the brink into penury. The only tools at hand for writing my telegram were a prehistoric pen and a pot of mildewed, virtually colourless ink the consistency of mud. With these I managed to scratch out the few words of abject apology that passed for my telegram and handed them over to a rather plain lady at the counter (let's be honest, to an incredibly ugly lady at the counter) who took it ungratefully, counted the words and snapped out a demand for money which I tossed back at her through the grille.

And I was about to retire from the premises in the healthy glow of a clear conscience when I suddenly stopped dead in my tracks; I had just noticed another employee of the Post Office sitting behind her, a young woman tapping away at a Morse transmitter with her back to me.

She was obviously young. She was even more obviously red-haired. And there was a good chance that she was pretty.

She had on a plain black dress which contribed to outline an attractively ample figure with nothing missing.

Her flowing hair was piled in coils on top of her head leaving the nape of her neck bare, and an angelic neck it was too, light golden brown with a little fleece of delicate down coming running down it and fading almost ethereally away into nothing.

Ah, if our souls ever grow hair, it will be hair like that!

Till suddenly I had an irrational, mad urge to plunge my lips into the pale golden hair of that telegraph operator.

In the hope that the young lady might turn round sooner or

later, I came back to the counter and engaged the old harridan in a long conversation about various Post Office services.

But the beautiful neck went on tapping out Morse, remorselessly.

And my friend Lenfileur began to get impatient.

So I left.

Anyone who knows me well will have guessed already that when the Post Office opened its doors for business next morning I was there waiting on the doorstep.

This time the beautiful redhead was on her own, which gave her no option but to show me her face. I had no complaints. It was well up to the standard set by her neck.

And what big dark eyes!

(Have you noticed what stunning dark eyes redheads sometimes have?)

I bought lots of stamps, sent lots of telegrams, asked after all the various local collection times and generally spent a good quarter of an hour giving a convincing imitation of an infatuated idiot.

She answered all my questions sweetly and reasonably, just like a sensible, well brought-up young girl.

After which I came back every day, and sometimes twice a day, because I soon found out exactly when she was on duty and took good care never to miss our little rendezvous, even if it was, sadly, only a rendezmoi.

To make these frequent visits seem plausible I had to write letters to all my friends and then, when I had run out of friends, to people I knew but didn't like.

After a while I found myself sending urgent telegrams to people I hardly knew and who must have thought I had gone out of my mind.

I cannot remember ever having embarked on such an orgy of correspondence.

And every time I turned up, I told myself: 'Right. This is it, This time you will declare your great passion.'

But each time I quailed before her businesslike air and instead of announcing straightforwardly: 'Mademoiselle, I love you!' all I could stammer was: 'Another three centime stamp, please, Mademoiselle.'

\* \* \*

It couldn't go on like this indefinitely.

Quite apart from anything else, I was due to go back to Paris very soon. So I decided to burn my boats and stake everything on one last final throw.

I arrived at the Post Office one morning and sent the following telegram to one of my friends:

*Coquelin Cadet, 17, Boulevard Haussmann, Paris.*
*I have fallen desperately in love with the little red-haired telegraph operator at Baisemoy-en-Cort Post Office. Please advise.*

I thought it might at the very least bring a faint blush to the unforgettable white cheeks of my loved one.

Not a bit of it.

With all the sang-froid in the world, she simply said:

'That will be ninety-five centimes, please, sir.'

Totally deflated by her majestic lack of interest, I summoned up just enough energy to delve in my pockets for the necessary. As it happened, I was completely out of small change. All I had on me was a 1,000-franc note.*

She took it from me, examined it carefully, felt it with her fingers . . . .

Obviously she was satisfied with her inspection because the prettiest smile imaginable suddenly spread across her features, revealing the most mouth-watering dimples in creation.

And then she slipped into the most common, not to say vulgar, of Parisian accents and said:

'Will you be needing your change back, sir?'


# COMFORT

I don't know about you, but I adore England. London, especially. Maybe it's because I'm a Parisian, but I love London town. I love its pubs, its music halls, its drunk old women in feathered hats. And the one thing which alone makes the journey worth the fare: the English concept of 'comfort'.

I would like to meet whoever it was who first circulated rumours of the Englishman's love of comfort. He must have a world-class sense of humour. The English love of comfort indeed! (Excuse me a moment, while I laugh up my sleeve.)

Not that *I* give a damn one way or the other about personal

* Don't look so surprised.

comfort. When you have been raised by a Spartan father, as I was, not to mention a Macedonian mother, you can do without it very well. If there are no napkins at table, I am quite happy to use the table-cloth. If I am given sheets on my bed no larger than a pocket handkerchief, no matter – I blow my nose on one, turn lightly on my heel and return the way I came, whistling a popular tune.

So much for comfort. And I have never had cause to complain. Yet, once . . .

(A warning to young, female, English readers: the following story is a little bit shocking . . .)

And yet, once, I confess, I would have liked to see a few more comforts laid on in London. That is, a few more conveniences. Because, as you probably know, London is most unlike Paris as far as the provision of public monuments for public relief is concerned. The monuments of Paris have given the word *bas-relief* to the world. In London there is no relief at all, however low.

And that evening I needed it badly. I had drunk a lot of ale, imbibed quite a bit of stout, and washed it all down with some porter. I was on my way back to my lodgings, about five or six o'clock, and as I walked down the Tottenham Court Road I suddenly became very nostalgic for the – well, the Boulevard Montmartre, for example. Because the Boulevard Montmartre is well lined with magazine kiosks, *colonnes Morris* and, above all, those comforting refuges which every Parisian is so used to having nearby.

The Tottenham Court Road may be a fine thoroughfare, but it completely lacks any such trappings of civilisation. Well, why not go into a building and ask for the concierge's help, do I hear you ask? Ah, wishful thinkers! There are no concierges in England. (Another example of their love of comfort.)

What could I do?

My ale, stout and porter had treacherously joined forces against me to plan a mass escape, and I felt I could not resist their efforts for long. But could I hold them off as far as Leicester Square? 'That was the question'.

I lengthened my stride. Acute agony brought me to a swift halt, and nailed me to the spot.

And then necessity became the mother of genius.

My eyes fell on a grand shop on which was blazoned, in letters of gold, these words: ALBERT FOX, Chemist and Druggist.

I don't know about you, but I adore English chemists' shops. I love the incredible variety of things they sell, the little sponges, the ties, the big sponges, the garters, the medium-sized sponges, etc., etc. . . .

So in I went resolutely.

'Good evening, sir,' said Albert Fox.

'Good evening,' I said, in Shakespeare's language, though not Shakespeare's words. 'I think I may have contracted diabetes.'

'Ah,' said the chemist (also in English).

'So I would like to make sure one way or the other.'

'That's quite simple, sir. All I need to do is analyse a sample of your . . . do you follow me?'

'Of course.'

And I did, into a little laboratory at the back, where he left me with a glass flask which had a funnel fixed at the top (for comfort, you understand). In no time at all, the flask had turned a bright amber colour in my hands. In fact – please don't get the idea that I am trying to show off, because I find the whole thing as revolting as you do – in fact the flask was not really big enough for the job and I was forced to add some more amber liquid to a dark potion bubbling away on a nearby burner.

When I reappeared, the chemist promised me faithfully to have the analysis scrupulously carried out by the same time the next day, so I left him with a cheery farewell and good night. But at that very same time the very next day you could have seen, on the steamer *Pétrel* bound full speed for Calais, the reclining, distinguished figure of a tall fair-haired young man killing himself with laughter over some private joke.

Well, if I ever do become a diabetic, I shall know that the god of English chemists has had his revenge.


## AN UNLIKELY STORY

I have just written to the editor of the *Journal Des Débats* to tell him that I have no option but to cancel my subscription. My reason for such an extreme action? Nothing less than the publication in his serious evening organ of a story so ludicrous that I myself would hesitate to put my name to it. Yet *they* have had the nerve to print it as coolly as if it were an everyday event. Well, when I buy the *Journal Des Débats*, I expect to get something serious to read for my money. You do too, don't you? Of course you do.

But when serious people like the staff of the *Journal Des Débats* decide to let their hair down, they don't do it by halves. And this time they have gone too far.

Anyway, judge for yourselves.

Here is the offending report, more or less word for word:—

'The distinguished Norwegian naturalist, Henrik Dahl of Talesund, a Darwinian scientist, recently decided to follow a living organism through all the stages of evolution.

'Accordingly, he bought a herring which had been caught alive in a Norwegian fjord and put it in an aquarium tank full of sea water. He renewed the water every day, but always replaced it with a slightly smaller quantity of liquid. As might be expected, this seemed to disturb the herring to begin with; eventually, though, he readjusted to the gradual loss of his maritime environment and began bit by bit to get used to an amphibious existence, living partly in air and partly in water.

'So M. Dahl took the experiment a stage further. He emptied *all* the water out of the tank. This naturally caused the herring some discomfort for a while, but he eventually recovered, adapted to his new dry surroundings, started breathing like a land animal and consequently found himself one rung higher on the ladder of evolution. As a reward, M. Dahl took him out of his glass prison and let him live on dry land, taking care to teach him to behave as befitted his new, dignified status. The herring, who turned out to be unusually intelligent, affectionate and adaptable, did all that was asked of him. He grew to like food that no fish had ever eaten before, he ate from his master's hand and at length became so fond of him that he was visibly depressed every time the latter had to go away on business.

'The time was obviously ripe for M. Dahl's fish, or animal, to climb yet another rung on the evolutionary ladder. This time he set out to teach him how to move about on land, and actually managed to get him slithering around like a snake. After a few months' practice the clever herring could actually move along quite fast – so much so that the scientist often took him for walks and led him around rather like a pet poodle.'

Well, to cut a long report short and get straight to the denouement . . .

'One day, M. Henrik Dahl and his faithful herring were strolling round the harbour area when they happened to pass over a bridge made of wooden slats laid loosely side by side. Sadly, the creature slipped through one of the cracks and fell into the water below.'

And, the *Journal Des Débats* adds coolly:

'It seems that the herring, being no longer used to sea water, was drowned immediately.'

## A SAD POEM TRANSLATED FROM THE BELGIAN
### for Maeterlinck

The woman I love will be an older woman, though not as
old as all that.
Having experienced everything that life can offer, she
will no longer believe in anything.
Though not beautiful, she will still have the ability to
enslave all men, without exception.
No-one has ever seen her laugh,
except, sometimes, when her pale mouth is touched by a
smile in memory of her tragic betrayals.

\*      \*      \*

Being the ex-mistress of an English painter who always
got cruelly drunk
and blackened her body
her whole body
with his blows,
she will have a healthy loathing for all men.

\*      \*      \*

She will deceive me with a young unpublished poet
whose hair, so long and thick
and not very clean,
will turn the heads of men in the street
and women as well

\*      \*      \*

I shall know all about it but, like a coward, pretend to
know nothing.

Nothing!

The young poet will dedicate his outpourings to me,
ironically.

*          *          *

The affair will last for months
and months.
Then one fine day, Eloa will become addicted to
morphine.

*          *          *

For Eloa is her name.

*          *          *

The morphine will wreak its usual havoc.
Eloa's cheeks will become pockmarked with little
blotches
and turn puffy,
so puffy
that her eyes will disappear
For hours on end she will lie on her sofa
like some great weary animal
and every time she breathes one will notice a strange
fetid odour.

*          *          *

One day, when Eloa's chemist is drunk,
he will make a mistake
and instead of morphine
give her some strange alkaline or other.
She will become as sick
as a dog.
Her extremities will go as cold
as those of a snake,
and the sound of agony will be heard in her throat.

*          *          *

Her suffering will get worse and worse.

*          *          *

I will put my hand into Eloa's hand
and she will make me swear
that when she is dead

I will kill myself.
That our two bodies, enclosed in the same bier,
will decompose and putrefy together.
The mingled juices of our rotting flesh will turn into
                                        the same sap,
feed the same stems of the same bushes,
flourish greenly in the same leaves
and spread, radiantly, into the same flowers.

\*          \*          \*

And in the cemetery,
in springtime,
when a young girl says: 'What a beautiful smell!'
that fragrance will be none other than the sublime
                    commingling of ours souls.

\*          \*          \*

These are the last wishes of Eloa.
I shall promise everything she asks, and more besides.

\*          \*          \*

Then she will die.

\*          \*          \*

I shall give Eloa a decent funeral and then,
next day,
I shall go out and get a mistress
who is a bit more fun.

## WIDOW AND SON

Once upon a time there lived at 256 rue Rougemont, in a nice
apartment on the second floor (3,500 francs a year, not counting
rates, etc.) a family who rejoiced in the name of Martin. There
were three of them: M. Martin, Mme Martin and their son, also
called M. Martin.

When our story begins, the father had just retired from business.
He had made a large fortune as the founder and chief director of
the *Society for Insurance against Solicitors*, despite which he was an

unusually retiring, not to say anti-social man, and (unlike his wife and child) cordially loathed all dances, evenings at the theatre and gatherings of any description. (His wife and child, who had no sense of respect whatsoever, were insufferably rude to him on this account.)

Mme Martin was on the wrong side of thirty, but partly made up for this by being on the right side of forty. As she was also rather pretty, dressed well and sparkled in company, many people took her to be her husband's daughter and her son's elder sister.

The son himself was eighteen and abominably spoilt by his mother. He had already fallen into bad habits and constantly borrowed large sums of money from friends of the family, ran up considerable debts with tradesmen and had even, on one occasion, touched the concierge for a small amount. Yet a mother's heart is infinitely forgiving and Mme Martin always repaid his debts, quite unknown to father.

But there came a day when young Martin got so deeply in debt that it could no longer be hid from Martin senior. And for once father completely lost his temper and laid down the law, to the effect that for his own good young Gaston should enlist in the Army for the next five years. Now, a mother's eyes contain infinite reservoirs of tears, and Mme Martin wept hard enough to flood the average landscape, but it was no good. M. Martin was made of granite. He was, in a word, adamant.

The only concession he made was that the distraught mother could accompany her son as far as the barracks. And there she burst into tears to such good effect that the platoon sergeant's heart softened and he advised her to go to the Captain or even the Colonel to plead for good treatment of her son.

She went to see the Captain first, a young buck of about thirty.

She stayed with him about a quarter of an hour and came out feeling a bit better.

Then she went to see the Colonel.

He was nearing sixty and, frankly, past his best.

Mme Martin stayed with him for about three quarters of an hour.

But she left him feeling much better.

Alas, it did not last for long, because when Gaston first wrote home he had heartbreaking news to report.

All the chocolate she had given him had been taken away.

And his description of military life was harrowing in the extreme – uncomfortable bedding, bad food, unsympathetic colleagues, unpleasant fatigue duties, tough training, practical jokes, tossings in blankets, etc. . . . The only nice thing about being in the army, it seemed, was listening to the regimental band on a Sunday afternoon.

Mme Martin could not stand the thought of her son's suffering. She took the next train and went to see the Colonel again. The Colonel was no older than he had been last time, but he hadn't got any younger either. So it was only after an hour of pleading by Mme Martin that he at last relented and agreed (quite against regulations) to let Private Martin have eight days' leave.

The next evening the family was reunited as before for the supper ritual; and talking things over, M. Martin admitted that he might have been a bit hasty in his decision. (A fine time to admit it!) Then, before he went to bed, M. Martin went out on the balcony to smoke his last pipe of the evening, as he always had done from time immemorial, while mother and son stayed to chat in the living room.

'Tell me,' said mother, 'is there really no way of getting out of this frightful regiment?'

'No, mother, not unless I am invalided out or become the son of a widow. That's the law.'

'Son of a widow?'

'Yes, mother, son of a widow.'

His mother thought things over for a moment, then said abruptly:

'Are you very fond of your father?'

'Of course not, mother! Are you?'

'Me?'

She raised her eyes heavenwards briefly. Then she said:

'I'll show you how fond I am. Just watch.'

At that very moment M. Martin was leaning right out over the edge of the balcony. His centre of gravity was not quite across the little railing, but it wasn't far off – any slight shift in the position of his mass might result in a highly unstable state of balance, not to say a sudden precipitation. Mme Martin crept up behind him, quiet as a vixen, grasped the seat of his trousers and smartly sent him on his way at high velocity towards the object on the pavement below which he had been studying so painstakingly, all executed with a precision and firmness which you might not have expected in such a society lady.

Meanwhile M. Martin was executing a brief but swift fall. At the very moment it ended he collided with a stretch of asphalt below, producing the kind of *whummmmmp!* noise made by meat when it is being flattened, followed almost instantaneously by a loud *crack!* as of clay being broken.

M. Martin's pipe had snapped in two.

Not only that, but a young lady walking past on the way back from the theatre found her dress splattered all over with grey blobs, which she started to wipe off with her handkerchief. But a kindly passer-by stopped and said:

'I wouldn't bother if I were you. It's only brain, and that doesn't mark clothes. Just let it dry and then tomorrow get it off with a good stiff brush. It won't leave a single trace.'

Which shows just how much the passer-by knew about it, because the human brain contains fatty matter (phosphorus) and stains clothes just like any other greasy stuff.

Meanwhile Mme Martin and her son had rushed down the stairs and come out to the scene of the accident.

'My husband!' shrieked the wife. 'Oh my poor, dear husband!'

'Father, father!' cried his son.

After which things took their usual course. A vast crowd gathered instantly, and bared their head out of respect for such doubly heartfelt grief. A fat doctor wheezed up, confirmed that M. Martin was dead and asked where he should send the bill to. A beautiful funeral was arranged for the late M. Martin, starring his son and heir in a lovely black outfit with a mourning band on his arm, sobbing so convulsively that everyone sighed: 'Poor, poor boy.' And there was a short legal ceremony which decided that M. Martin had been killed by a fall caused by a fit of apoplexy.

After which, being now a widow's son, young Martin quickly left the Army and became a civilian again, much to the anguish of the Colonel who had become hugely attracted to Mme Martin.

Sorry though I feel for the bereaved pair, I cannot conceal that the period of mourning observed by the widow and orphan was remarkably short. After what might seem an indecently brief interval they swung back into society again, showing either a distressing lack of taste or a remarkable philosophical resignation.

But the best bit of the story is that Mme Martin has, with the full backing of her son, decided to remarry, and is shortly to become a wife again. Which means, though it has not occurred to either of them, that Gaston will promptly be recalled to the ranks again.

The only person who might warn them is the Colonel, and he has no intention of letting them know. He would rather wait and see Gaston's expression when he is re-enlisted.

# THE POLYMYTH

I first set eyes on him in a café in the Latin Quarter when he came in and sat down at the table next to me. And ordered six cups of coffee.

'Aha,' I thought to myself. 'This gentleman is about to be joined by five friends, if I am not much mistaken.'

I was much mistaken. As soon as the six cups of steaming Mocha had arrived he drank them all himself, one after the other. (Which is much the best way to do it, as you will know if you have ever tried to drink six cups of coffee simultaneously.) When he noticed my air of bafflement, he leant across to enlighten me.

'It's quite simple,' he said. (He spoke in a flat, down-at-heel sort of voice, as if he was talking with his shoe-laces undone.) 'The fact is, I am another Balzac. I, too, drink far too much coffee.'

Fascinated, I waited to see what he would do next. I didn't have to wait long. He called the waiter over and asked him to bring some writing paper. As soon as it came, he scribbled a few words on the first sheet, then crumpled it and threw it under the table. The same happened to the next. And the next. And the next and the next, until the floor was covered in screwed up pieces of paper.

'You see,' he told me in the same flat voice, 'you see, I am another Flaubert. I find it almost impossible to get a sentence right.'

Such a distinguished man was obviously worth cultivating and in order to find out more about him, I struck up a conversation. But when I happened to mention that I was a Norman from Honfleur, it brought a deep frown to his face.

'I am sorry to hear that. I am like Charlemagne; I despise the barbarians from the north.'

I hastily explained that we Normans had ceased being Norsemen many years ago, and he looked relieved at the news.

'Ah, I didn't know that. I know nothing about the north – as a matter of fact, I am another Puvis de Chavannes. I too grew up in Lyons.'

Where, it turned out, all his family had been in the meat trade. In fact, his father had insisted on his going into the business for a while.

'I am another Shakespeare. I too started out as a butcher's boy.'

Then he had moved to Paris, fallen in love and got married. He didn't tell me very much about his wife.

'Let's just say that I have much in common with the Emperor Napoleon I. We both married a woman called Josephine.'

Josephine, sad to say, had run off almost immediately with an Englishman, leaving my friend feeling somewhat hurt, not to say rather offended.

'Put it this way,' he put it. 'I am another Molière. I too had an unfaithful wife.'

Part of the trouble seems to have been that he and Josephine were not entirely compatible in some ways. She, apparently, liked very virile, very passionate men. Unfortunately . . .

'You see, I have something else in common with Napoleon. My . . . .'

The rest of the sentence was carried away by a sudden gust of wind. Being very anxious to learn more about a man with so many diverse talents, I was careful not to leave before I had arranged to meet him again, and we agreed to have lunch together soon, fixing our rendezvous for twelve midday precisely.

I arrived at one minute past twelve and found him tapping his watch impatiently.

'You may not have realised that I am another Louis XIV. I cannot bear to be kept waiting.'

He relented sufficiently over lunch to tell me in great detail about a serious eye infection he had been suffering from since I last saw him. Luckily the doctors had found a cure and now it had almost completely cleared up. Or as he put it, with a slight variation on the normal theme:

'I have no wish to be another Homer or Milton.'

The other news he had at this, our second meeting, was that he had managed to shake off the memory of Josephine by falling in love with another woman.

Alas, I heard some time later that she had not returned his feelings and had rejected all his overtures.

So he had shot her dead.

And they had arrested him for murder.

When he first came to court, he refused to answer any of the examining magistrate's questions.

'I am very sorry,' he told him. 'I am afraid I am another Louis XV. I do not recognise the authority of this court.'

Which did not prevent him, in due course, from coming up for trial.

I'm glad to say that this time he did speak up for himself.

'I wish to say in my defence that I am a second Attila the Hun. I am a law unto myself.'

The jury did not consider this to be an extenuating circumstance and passed sentence of death on him. The only thing that could have saved him then was a Presidential reprieve but, as usual, our head of state was surrounded by incompetent advisers and no Presidential reprieve was forthcoming.

Poor boy. I can still remember clearly the third and last time I saw him. He came through the prison gates at dawn like a pale Pierrot, with his hands tied behind his back, his feet bound and his shirt slashed at the top in a conveniently guillotine-shaped cut. I was standing among the onlookers, and he turned round and saw me.

He smiled then, and spoke the last words I ever heard him say in that flat voice which sounded as if he were talking with his shoe-laces undone.

'I am another Jesus Christ. We were both fated to die at the age of thirty-three.'


# A MOST UNUSUAL WAY TO DIE

The highest recorded tide of this century (the fifteenth I have witnessed personally and many more to come, I hope) took place last Tuesday, November 6.

It was a fine sight and I wouldn't have missed it for all the tea in China. Or India. Or, indeed, Ceylon.

The sea was very rough that day; whipped on by a strong S.W. wind, it rose to quay-top level at Le Havre and flooded into the drains of the said town, meeting the inhabitants' waste water half-way along and obligingly taking it back into their houses.

All the doctors rubbed their hands with glee.

'Good, good!' they said. 'Lots of lovely typhoid fever!'

For – can you believe it? – the town of Le Havre is built in such a way that its drains are above sea level and after every little high tide that comes along you can see the intimate rubbish of the men of Le Havre cynically displayed along the main streets.

(You might, in parenthesis, think that that swine François I could have spent less time drinking and whoring, and more time doing something about maintaining the highways and byways of his kingdom.) *

Never mind – it was a fine sight.

I spent the best part of the day on the jetty watching boats come in and boats go out. When the wind started blowing even harder I turned up the collar of my overcoat and was about to do the same for the bottom of my trousers (I like to keep things symmetrical) when my friend Axelsen appeared.

My friend Axelsen is a young Norwegian painter, with lots of talent and lots of sentimental ideas.

He is very talented when he is sober. The rest of the time he is just sentimental.

At this particular moment he seemed to be in one of his sentimental periods. Whether it was the effect of the strong wind or because his heart was overflowing, I don't know, but his eyes were undoubtedly brimming with tears.

'Well, well,' I cried cheerfully. 'Something wrong, Axelsen?'

'No, everything's fine. It's a marvellous sight. It just brings back sad memories, that's all. Whenever I see the highest recorded tide of the century, the memory breaks my heart.'

'Memory of what? Tell me about it.'

'I'd be glad to. Not here, though.'

And so saying, he dragged me into the back-room of a local tobacconist's where a pretty young English girl produced a *swenska-punch* from nowhere for us.

Axelsen staunched his tears and told me the following tragic tale.

'It all happened about five years ago, when I was just starting out as an artist and was living in Bergen (Norway). One day, evening rather, I went to a ball given by M. Isdahl the big cod roe exporter, and there I met and fell in love with a lovely young girl who in turn seemed not unattracted to me. As you can imagine, it wasn't long before I got an introduction to her father and soon I was accepted as a friend of the family.

'Well, I found out one day that her birthday was coming up soon and decided I ought to give her a very special sort of present. The trouble was: what? Now, you know the Bay of Vaagen . . . .'

---

* If a descendant of that monarch should happen to read these lines and take offence, he need only come and find me. I have never shrunk from an encounter with a Valois.

'Not terribly well . . . .'

'Oh, it's a bay near Bergen. The point was, my girlfriend was very fond of it, especially one little corner of it. So I had the bright idea of painting a pretty little water-colour of that particular spot. "That should please her," I thought. And off I set one fine morning with my water-colour set.

'There was just one thing I had forgotten to take along with me: water. I'm sure you know that whereas in some trades it is frowned on to add water to one's goods (viniculture springs to mind), it is virtually de rigueur for a water-colourist. And I hadn't got any! Well, dammit, I thought, I'll use *sea* water for my water-colour and see how it turns out.

'It turned out very well. I came back with an excellent little painting which I presented in due course to my girl and which she in turn duly hung up in her bedroom. The only thing was . . . . Do you know what had happened?'

'I will when you tell me.'

'What had happened was that the part of the painting which depicted the sea, being largely sea water, was subject to the attraction of the moon and therefore tidal. Which meant, strange as it may seem, that you could see the sea in my painting coming up, up, up over the rocks by the shore's edge and going down, down, down, leaving them high and dry again at low tide.'

'Ah!'

'Exactly. And one night we had the highest recorded tide of the century, just like today. The coast of Norway was swept by the most fearful storms. It thundered, it rained, it blew, it did everything.

'And in the morning I went over to the villa where my girlfriend lived, only to find the whole household in a state of utter despair.

'My water-colour had overflowed during the night and drowned her as she slept.'

'My poor young friend!'

Axelsen was weeping like a baby. I clasped his hand.

'You know,' he said, 'it's all true what I've told you, every single word of it. If you don't believe me, ask Johanson.'

I happened to bump into Johanson that very evening. I asked him about the episode. He assured me that every single word of it was a complete leg-pull.

# NO HURRY

Can you think of anything more stupid than the average proverb?
I can't. In fact, if any reader can come up with something more
stupid, I will send him free and gratis half a kilo of fresh juicy
English cherries (which have just come into season).

On second thoughts, I shall have to withdraw my wonderful
free offer, because I have just thought of something more stupid
than the average proverb. No, no, not the old music hall joke,
'Two average proverbs'. Something just a bit more sophisticated,
namely 'Two average proverbs side by side'.

For instance, 'Too many cooks spoil the broth' beside 'Many
hands make light work'. You see?

Here's another pair. 'More haste, less speed' and 'A stitch in time
saves nine'. It just doesn't add up, does it? Of course it doesn't.

When it comes to haste and speed, anyway, I don't need any
help from proverbs, because I worked out a suitable philosophy
for the true pace of life when I was still a toddler. (All disbelieving
letters will gladly be forwarded to my mother for refutation.) It
was, quite simply, always to put off to the day after tomorrow
anything that could easily have been done the day before yesterday. And it works. If you take my advice and *never* hurry, you will
succeed in life. Think of all those people who have gone to an
early grave because they hurried. If I had always hurried, I would
be dead now as I write these words. (What a loss to the world!)
But no – I have always taken my time never hurried and now here
I am, happy, contented and alive.

Let me tell you the full, fascinating story.

\*　　　\*　　　\*

When I first came to Paris I was a young man clutching a small
legacy in my hot little hand, so not unnaturally my first ex-
cursion was an evening out in the Latin Quarter. It lasted about
a year. At the end of that time my resources had shrunk so small
that they could not have been measured by any known scientific
instrument. You see, I had met a tall blonde girl who worked
as a waitress at the Brasserie Lapin Mauve and who had a great
weakness for champagne .... I know what you're thinking.

You're thinking I spent all my money on champagne for her. You misjudge me. Only half of it went that way. (The other half I spent on a ravishing brunette who had a weakness for dry curaçao . . . .)

One day I stumbled on the great economic truth that the best way to save money is to stop buying people champagne and dry curaçao, but it was just too late. I had already spent all my money. Not only that, but I had also acquired many bad habits and succumbed to an allergy for hard work. The position was hopeless. So I decided to take my own life . . . but not just yet.

I woke up one morning fully determined to end it all, as I did most mornings, only to find in the post a letter telling me of the death of a distant uncle. I hadn't seen him since childhood, hadn't ever thought about him much, hadn't even liked him. And yet who do you think was his sole heir? Yes, me. And how! You see, my uncle had been a big pig breeder somewhere in the Auge valley, and pig breeding is *the* way to make money. All you have to do is spend two sous on a tiny baby pig, then relieve your neighbours of all their scraps, crusts and peelings and stuff them into your porker till it grows into a profitable monster which you can sell to a pork butcher for a cool 3,000 francs. Then the pork butcher takes his big knife . . . .

I'm sure you don't want to hear about the murderous habits of pork butchers. All you need know is that nothing in a pig has to be thrown away unsold, so my uncle had made a small fortune. Which I immediately made a start on (o–60 in three seconds). Not in the Latin Quarter this time, though. Oh, no. This time I bought my way into high society where gentlemen are very much gentlemen, very well-behaved and, as I found to my cost, very much inclined to let you foot the bill for the refreshments.

And once more I sat broke and toying with the idea of a quick, painless death in the near future. Not all pig breeders were uncles of mine, unfortunately, and even if they had been, pig breeders don't die every day. Far from it, as a matter of fact. Smile if you like, but they don't come much tougher than the average pig breeder. Well, think of the life they have to lead. Up at two or three every morning, travelling in all weathers, traipsing from town to town, market to market . . . . Think you could do the job all right, do you? Don't make me laugh. You wouldn't last more than three weeks at the outside.

Where were we? Oh yes. I was bankrupt again, this time hopelessly. I had to sell my furniture, sell my books, sell everything until finally I was left with nothing but my revolver. So on the day when my very last sou had disappeared I opened my mouth, inserted the gun into this convenient opening . . . and suddenly thought:

'I must be mad! Fancy committing suicide with a weapon worth at least a hundred francs. I can surely raise some money on it. We'll have another think about things after that. There's still plenty of time.'

I found an old pawnbroker who, after a lot of haggling, offered me ten francs on my pistol. I took it. Just as a precaution, I used twenty sous out of the ten francs to buy a good length of rope; a nice bit of rope it was too, stout yet not too thick, strong but very pliable. I almost felt tempted to use it there and then, for the sheer pleasure of it, but not quite.

Well, the rest of the ten francs kept me alive for three days, me and the rope, because I quickly grew inseparable from it as a sort of good luck charm. But on the third day I finally decided that the moment had really come to end it all and I went back to my rooms clutching my trusty rope. And who should I find waiting for me but my friendly landlady? Kindly she explained that as I was now owing more than a month's rent she would be grateful to have my key back and smilingly took it from me.

My rope and I sallied forth into the night once more, promising we would be back soon with the rent money.

A nasty night it was too, much too nasty for suicide by drowning. All night I walked beside the Seine, so black, so silent, so tempting, yet so freezing cold. At last the light of day returned. So did my appetite. I went back to the pawnbroker and parted tearfully with my rope for which he gave me two sous, on condition I threw in my waistcoat buttons as well.

I managed to survive the rest of the day on a plate of vegetable soup for which I paid my entire fortune.

\*      \*      \*

Evening returned. My last evening on earth, I thought to myself.

For a long time I wandered along the quays and over the bridges, postponing the final moment as usual.

Then suddenly I thought – well, here goes, goodbye everyone and happy landings.

Splash!

\*      \*      \*

I had no sooner landed in the water than I heard another *splash* quite close to me, almost like an echo of mine.

'That's nice!' I thought. 'A dog has leapt in to save me.'

I swam towards the sound to make his job easier.

I'm glad I did, because, far from being a charitable dog, it was a woman thrashing round in the water. Obviously another suicide attempt like me.

'Hello, there might be a reward going here . . . .' I thought, and swam faster.

Moments later I had pulled her out on to the bank and was reviving her with some heartfelt friction. She came to and looked round her.

'Where am I?' she said. 'Oh no! I've been saved! And I so wanted to die!'

'I'm very sorry,' I said, somewhat abashed.

'It doesn't matter,' she said, and fainted again. Things were taken out of my hands at that moment because an officer of the law galloped up, puffing hard and took over the resuscitation. When she came round for the second time and sat up, he told her that he had seen everything that happened.

'This man saved your life,' he said gravely.

She held out her hand to me and smiled sadly.

'Thank you,' she said. 'You weren't to know.' She was certainly very pretty, my sad little half-drowned girl, very pale, with long black hair and great big beautiful shy eyes.

And presently, summoned by the police, her parents arrived, both very upset and in a great state. Her mother turned out to be a harpy of the worst kind and hardly gave me a second glance, but her father took me warmly and gratefully in his arms. It was from him that I learnt the whole story – how the young girl had been desperately in love with a young man who had led her on, how he had run off and abandoned her, how she had immediately tried to take her own life, and how only my prompt action could have saved her.

As it turned out, her midnight bathe had done a great deal to cool her passion. In fact – I have to tell you this – she promptly fell in love again, but this time with the man who had rescued her.

Me.

And we are now very happily married.

I hope you agree now that my lifelong habit of leaving everything to the last moment paid off handsomely.

What else can I tell you?

Only that I still love my wife and that my mother-in-law died last week.

# HOW FAR CAN THE BOOK PUBLICITY PEOPLE GO, ALWAYS ASSUMING, THE WAY THINGS ARE GOING AT THE MOMENT, THAT THEY WILL EVER STOP?

The other day I was feeling pretty seedy.

The heat, perhaps. Or chronic indigestion. I don't know. What I do know is that I was feeling pretty seedy.

And when I feel seedy I tend to do the most extraordinary and baroque things.

Which explains how I came to be deep in scrutiny of the classified advertisements on the back of *Le Journal* (the most stylish and best informed newspaper in all Paris. Well, the only one with six pages anyway).

And there it was that I came across the following reviving lines:

*Small fortune guaranteed within a month, no risk involved. New system, open to all. Write to Box 27, c/o Le Journal.*

Small fortune, eh? How about that, I thought. Not that I wouldn't have preferred a large one, but as there didn't seem to be any choice on offer I simply took pen in hand and wrote off to Box 27 saying how much I was looking forward to our future relationship.

I had hardly returned to the paper when an even more extraordinary advertisement caught my eye:

*Young deaf and dumb girl, dowry 1,700,000 francs, wishes meet man of the world, view white marriage. Write to Lucia H.W. c/o Le Journal.*

'How about *that*!' I thought. 'A wife with 1,700,000 francs is a bit of all right, but a *dumb* wife . . .! Quick – pen and paper!'

So I wrote a passionate letter to Lucia H.W., not forgetting to slip into the envelope a distinguished photostudy of my good self . . . . It was obviously my lucky day because the next advertisement I looked at was every bit as good as the first two:

*Amazing! Amazing! Amazing! My methods cure all diseases and ailments! Write to Dr. 2,119, c/o Le Journal.*

Amazed, amazed, amazed, I sent off a letter to the good Dr 2,119. And while I was at it I replied to two other advertisements:

*Free country holiday for a month, in return for a little light work. Write to BK, 19, Le Journal.*

And, somewhat more mysteriously:

*Blkw sqkrs ljxrb sss bcd. Write: RSPZ, Journal.*

Feeling much better after all this exercise, I ordered a second bottle of wine and ended up later that evening lying on a bench in one of the better boulevards, happily dreaming of small fortunes, white marriages, perfect health, country junkets and blkw sqkrs.

I need hardly tell you, though, that I was up bright and early the next morning, waiting with the concierge for the postman.

And there were five letters for me!

Feverishly, I tore open the first one.

Only to read:

'Sir, to make a fortune in a month all you have to do is write a book as good as *With my Heart on my Sleeve and my Stomach in my Socks*, by Edouard Osmont, now at all good bookshops.'

Just my luck, I thought. A leg-pull.

The deaf and dumb heiress replied as follows:

'Why don't you stop chasing women, you dirty old man, and do something worthwhile like reading Edouard Osmont's new book, *With my Heart on my Sleeve and my Stomach in my Socks?*'

Not again! I began to suspect a conspiracy.

The third letter read:

'Cure all your ills by reading *With my Heart on my Sleeve and my Stomach in my Socks*, by Edouard Osmont.'

I opened the fourth letter with a certain foreboding.

'You could quickly earn enough for a holiday in the country if you wrote a book like *With my Heart on my Sleeve and my Stomach in my Socks* by Edouard Osmont.'

Only a profound sense of duty enabled me to unseal the fifth and last envelope.

'Blkw *With my Heart* sqkrs *on my Sleeve and my Stomach* ljxrb *in my Socks* by Edouard Osmont.'

*     *     *

That funny noise? It is the sound of great French authors turning in their graves.